Serious Fun

How Guided Play Extends Children's Learning

Marie L. Masterson & Holly Bohart EDITORS

National Association for the Education of Young Children

Washington, DC

naeyc®

National Association for the Education of Young Children
1313 L Street NW, Suite 500
Washington, DC 20005-4101
202-232-8777 • 800-424-2460
NAEYC.org

NAEYC Books

Senior Director, Publishing and Professional Learning
Susan Friedman

Editor in Chief
Kathy Charner

Senior Editor
Holly Bohart

Editor
Rossella Procopio

Senior Creative Design Manager
Henrique Siblesz

Senior Creative Design Specialist
Charity Coleman

Creative Design Specialist
Malini Dominey

Publishing Business Operations Manager
Francine Markowitz

Through its publications program, the National Association for the Education of Young Children (NAEYC) provides a forum for discussion of major issues and ideas in the early childhood field, with the hope of provoking thought and promoting professional growth. The views expressed or implied in this book are not necessarily those of the Association.

The following selections were previously published in the specified issues of *Young Children*: B. Hassinger-Das, K. Hirsh-Pasek, and R.M. Golinkoff, "The Case of Brain Science and Guided Play: A Developing Story," May 2017; D. Stipek, "Playful Math Instruction in the Context of Standards and Accountability," July 2017; P. McDonald, "Observing, Planning, Guiding: How an Intentional Teacher Meets Standards Through Play," March 2018; B. Ripstein, "'There's a Story in My Picture!' Connecting Art, Literacy, and Drama through Storytelling in a Kindergarten Classroom," March 2018; D. Davis and D. Farran, "Positive Early Math Experiences for African American Boys: Nurturing the Next Generation of STEM Majors," May 2018; S. Riley-Ayers and A. Figueras-Daniel, "Engaging and Enriching: The Key to Developmentally Appropriate Academic Rigor," May 2018.

The following selections were previously published in the specified issues of *Teaching Young Children*: C. Ward, "Preschoolers Play with Bamboo," October/November 2016; I. Salinas-Gonzalez, M. Arreguín-Anderson, and I. Alanís, "Supporting Language: Culturally Rich Dramatic Play," December/January 2018; L. Bongiorno, "Talking with Parents about Play and Learning," August/September 2018.

Photo Credits

Contents

In this book you'll encounter a range of ways teachers can enhance preschoolers' and kindergartners' learning through playful instruction. How do you see the fit between play and learning for children?

Thought-provoking questions and comments at the beginning of each chapter prime you to critically reflect on the authors' viewpoints and what it might look like to guide children's play.

Introduction

Marie L. Masterson and Holly Bohart

What kind of experiences best support young children's learning? In the last several decades, we've learned a great deal about how children learn and develop, and research shows that play is a key way they discover, build, and reinforce knowledge about their world (Langford 2010; Tayler 2015). For 3- to 6-year-olds, play may be a child dancing to his favorite song or telling stories to a rapt audience of stuffed animals; a few children running a bakery with materials the teacher has provided based on her careful observation of the children's interests; and several children playing a card game first with rules explained by their teacher, and then gradually adapting the game with their own rules. Sometimes play is entirely child selected and directed; in other situations, adults provide scaffolding in a playful setting to nurture children's emerging capabilities and knowledge. Although these examples range from unstructured play to guided play to playing games, all are play, and all involve learning.

Consider some of the many ways children benefit from unstructured and other types of play:

> Fosters social skills (Ramani 2012; Ramani & Eason 2015)

> Enhances self-regulation and executive function (Becker et al. 2014; Cavanaugh et al. 2017; Christie & Roskos 2009; McCrory, De Brito, & Viding 2010; Ramani & Brownell 2014; Savina 2014)

> Improves language skills (Cohen & Emmons 2017; Ramani 2012; Ramani & Eason 2015; Stagnitti et al. 2016)

> Supports math and science learning (Bulotsky-Shearer et al. 2014; Cohen & Emmons 2017; Trawick-Smith, Swaminathan, & Liu 2016)

> Provides health and physical benefits such as healthy body weight, increased coordination, improved sleep, and reduced stress and anxiety (Levine & Ducharme 2013; Wenner 2009)

According to the American Academy of Pediatrics (AAP), "play is not frivolous; it is brain building. Play has been shown to have both direct and indirect effects on brain structure and functioning" (Yogman et al. 2018, 5). Clearly, play is a powerful force for enhancing children's well-being, development, and success in school and in life.

Guiding Children's Learning Through Playful Experiences

Play can be thought of as a spectrum that includes free play, guided play, and games (Zosh et al. 2018). Children learn as they engage in unstructured play as well as other types of play, including those that are initiated and guided by the teacher. The ideas in this book focus primarily on "playful learning—a whole-child pedagogical approach to the promotion of academic, socio-emotional, and cognitive development" (Toub et al. 2018). Each chapter outlines how teachers playfully combine children's interests with learning opportunities and goals. To deepen children's learning, teachers skillfully support children as they pursue activities of their own choosing and also introduce specific learning goals in the context of playful, enjoyable experiences.

Research suggests that play most effectively supports learning when children have opportunities for both free play and guided play (Honomichi & Chen 2012; Weisberg et al. 2016). *Guided play* experiences provide adult scaffolding in the context of activities that young children find engaging and motivating. As Weisberg and colleagues (2016) explain, guided play has two components:

> Child autonomy: Children direct their own play and exploration

> Adult guidance: Teachers set up the environment and use open-ended comments and suggestions to nudge children toward a learning goal while still providing children with choices

As you will see from the chapters in this book, there are a variety of ways to balance child initiation and choice with intentional adult scaffolding that adds to children's present knowledge and abilities. There are also many ways this balance is referred to. In this book, you'll see *guided play* and *playful learning* along with other terms. While not synonymous, the terms describe some intentional combination of child-directed play and teacher guidance. Some of the authors present ways teachers can deepen children's learning as they support play and build on children's ideas; other authors present playful learning situations that involve more teacher guidance, like math games. Playful instruction looks different depending on your goals for children, the situation, and individual children's abilities and interests.

It can be challenging to embed teacher-guided, content-rich activities into play-based experiences. In *Serious Fun*, more than a dozen authors—teachers, teacher educators, researchers, and consultants—share their thoughts and the research on how educators can provide playful activities that enhance preschool and kindergarten children's knowledge and skills.

> Learning may appear to be spontaneous in such settings, but activities and interactions are intentionally designed to integrate language and academic concepts in ways that build on the funds of knowledge that each child brings, reflecting the child's individual social identities and her family's language, culture, and experiences.

Carefully evaluating your teaching practices and intentionally guiding children's play can result in deep, rich learning for children.

The benefits of guided play are not limited to children. As you make continual shifts in your classroom role between leader and play facilitator to best support children's abilities and needs, providing an environment and activities that are appropriately challenging and flexible, you free yourself to support children's overall development (see McDonald, Chapter 2).

Support for Playful Learning

The information, guidance, and strategies presented by the authors of these chapters align with several statements issued by or forthcoming from professional bodies: the AAP report on the power of play; NAEYC's forthcoming position statement on equity and diversity; and "Standards and Competencies for Early Childhood Educators," an NAEYC position statement that is undergoing revision at the time of this writing.

The American Academy of Pediatrics Report on the Power of Play

The content of this book is grounded in biological, brain, and educational research that substantiates the essential role of play in healthy child development. *The Power of Play: A Pediatric Role in Enhancing Development in Young Children*, the 2018 report by the AAP (Yogman et al. 2018), states that active play is fundamental to children's health and is an essential foundation for the skills they will need to live successful lives in a complex world. Play helps children learn to cooperate, solve problems, negotiate, and develop leadership skills and creativity, and it ensures a strong start in language and cognitive skills. Play experiences decrease anxiety in children and may serve as a buffer for toxic stress, especially with the safety and support of a nurturing adult. The report encourages early childhood programs to ensure a balanced curriculum that includes playful learning to promote healthy development.

NAEYC's Position Statement on Equity and Diversity

As teachers provide joyful, meaningful learning opportunities for children, they must actively work to instill principles of fairness and justice that reflect the goals of anti-bias education. Teachers build on each child's unique set of individual and family strengths, cultural background, language, abilities, and experiences. As they take care not to impose their own personal and cultural preferences and biases on children, they seek to find ways to equitably support each child's development and learning.

For example, the NAEYC position statement on equity and diversity in early childhood education (NAEYC, forthcoming a) calls attention to the emerging research base on implicit bias, which reveals, among other findings, that white teachers view the play of children of color, particularly African American boys, differently than that of other children (Yates & Marcelo 2014).

> Teachers must recognize and mediate bias and barriers in all areas of teaching to ensure that all children experience needed cognitive, social, and linguistic advantages that prepare them for future success in school and in life.

Teachers should understand their role in facilitating learning in playful situations and work toward these goals through conversation, understanding the children and families they work with, providing culturally and developmentally appropriate experiences and interactions, and ensuring the highest level of achievement for all children. These early experiences are necessary to help children overcome early gaps in achievement and ensure long-term school success.

A sense of familiarity, ownership, and engagement is needed for children to feel safe and supported. Children who feel connected to the setting, to you, and to play experiences take pride in learning. This is essential to their motivation and feelings of competence. They develop a sense of belonging and confidence in trying new things and taking risks necessary to grow.

NAEYC Professional Standards and Competencies for Early Childhood Educators

NAEYC's standards and competencies for early childhood professionals focus on what teachers of young children should know and be able to do to support all areas of development, including "physical, cognitive, social, emotional, linguistic, and aesthetic domains: critical elements of brain development; learning motivation, social interaction, and play" (Standard 1, NAEYC, forthcoming b). Effective teachers understand theory and research and can provide challenging and achievable experiences for each child through play, spontaneous interactions and exploration, and guided investigations, based on their knowledge about "developmentally appropriate, culturally and linguistically relevant, universally designed materials and environments for early education" (Standards 4 and 5). They continue to learn by working with colleagues and growing in their knowledge (Standard 6). *Serious Fun* offers practical, effective support for teachers to ground learning in play and gain a deeper understanding of their role in facilitating playful learning experiences. In addition, the research and reasoning presented provide a solid base for advocating for play as vital to children's development and learning.

About this Book

In Part 1, you'll explore how extending children's learning through playful activities promotes higher-level thinking and planning and the emerging brain science that suggests why guided play is a promising approach. The classroom examples and supporting research show how an intentionally created play environment fosters problem solving, creativity, and persistence and helps children meet content standards. You'll gain insight into the factors that are necessary for weaving together play and learning standards.

Part 2 describes content-rich activities that build on children's natural curiosity to explore and make sense of the world, examining questions like the following: What does "playful math" look like, and why is it more effective than worksheets and flashcards? How do you consider and build on children's social and cultural backgrounds as you plan literacy and math activities? How can teachers use a unique material in ways that sustain children's interest and grow their learning and social skills over an entire year? How can programs and schools put children at the center of learning, focusing not only on academic content but also on approaches to learning?

Engage with the ideas presented throughout the book, considering children's roles as active agents in their own learning and your own role in setting high expectations for children and helping them meet those expectations.

When you invite children into playful learning experiences, you are not "just letting [them] play" (McDonald, page 23, this volume). You are creating an intentional, responsive learning environment that is based on your understanding of how children learn, what they know and understand now, and what they want and need to learn next—and you anticipate spontaneous, joyful discoveries with them along the way.

Suggested strategies at the end of each chapter will help you apply the ideas to your own teaching.

Try This!

› Use the reflection questions on page 113 to consider and evaluate your own setting. To learn more, investigate some of the additional resources suggested by the authors ("Resources for Further Reading," page 127). Use the reproducible resource on pages 116–117 to explain to families what children learn from play.

› As you explore the chapters, think about how *you* see the fit between play and learning for the children you work with. In Chapter 5, Deborah Stipek notes that "standards provide useful goalposts, but only the children themselves can show you where to start" (page 62). Learn from the children. Reflect with your colleagues, and work with them to implement strategies from this book. Together, you can integrate active play with challenging learning goals in your setting.

PART ONE

Intentionally Creating Play Environments for Learning

Drawing from discoveries from both brain science and behavioral research, the authors of this chapter argue that free play and guided play—together called *playful learning*—can be a dynamic combination of tools for supporting children's development in ways that are enjoyable but also conceptually rich. Consider the definition of guided play presented, and think about why this strategy can be such a powerful learning tool. What is your reaction to the authors' ideas? How does guided play seem to enhance children's enjoyment of play and what they are learning as they experiment with materials and interact with others? Might it potentially interfere with children's agency? If so, what are some ways to more seamlessly balance free play and guided play?

1

Brain Science and Guided Play

Brenna Hassinger-Das, Kathy Hirsh-Pasek, and Roberta Michnick Golinkoff

Ms. Elena's Head Start classroom is filled with eager 3- and 4-year-olds. It's center time, and the children have split into small groups. At one center, Ms. Elena has carefully selected play materials—including a barn, a chicken coop, and animal figurines—that reflect the story lines and specific vocabulary words from books related to farm life she read aloud as part of the class's storybook theme of the week. While Ms. Elena looks on, Sara, Javon, and Ashish arrive at the center and immediately pick up the toys. They each choose a figurine and begin playing. Sara says to Javon, "I'll be the cow!" Javon says, "Okay, then I'll be the chicken. I'm going to go sleep in the coop. The cow should go sleep in the barn." Ashish says, "Then I'll be the horse, and I'll go sleep in the barn too."

Together, the three children move their figurines to the coop and the barn while making mooing, clucking, and neighing sounds. Since coop was one of the week's focus words, Ms. Elena joins in the children's play, making sure that Sara and Ashish understand the word as well as Javon does: "Sleeping in the coop sounds like a great idea, Javon! A coop is a house for chickens. Remember when we saw a coop on our field trip to Maple Farm? Javon, Sara, and Ashish, where do you think the chickens would live if we didn't have a coop on the farm?" Ashish says, "I think they live in the barn!" Then Sara says, "Yes, they live in the barn, because it's nice and warm inside there." Ms. Elena says, "That sounds like a really good place for the chickens to live if we didn't have a coop!"

At this point, Ms. Elena steps back and the children take up a new direction for the play. She continues to listen for ways to build on the children's interests and reinforce their weekly focus words during the session without interrupting their play.

Why Play?

Monkeys play. Dogs play. Rats play. Even octopuses play. And without any instruction, children of all races and genders, in all cultures of the world, invent and reinvent play in every generation. Something this ubiquitous must provide evolutionary advantages to both animals and humans. Decades of research suggest just that. In particular, free play and guided play—together known as *playful learning*—are pedagogical tools through which children can learn in joyful and conceptually rich ways, as is evident in the opening vignette. Brain science research in animals has left clues along a path that may begin to reveal play's human biological underpinnings, but more research is needed to investigate *why* play promotes learning and development.

From Animal Brains to Children's Behavior

Perhaps the most striking finding about play comes from research with animals in which play—specifically, rough-and-tumble play—has been shown to promote early brain development. For example, playful rats act more appropriately in social situations than rats that do not play (Burgdorf, Panksepp, & Moskal 2011). These findings offer a potential model of how play may help develop children's social functioning and brain architecture.

A growing body of behavioral research establishes relationships between children's play and development in several areas, including language (Toub et al. 2018), executive functions (Tominey & McClelland 2011), mathematics and spatial skills (Fisher et al. 2013), scientific thinking (Schulz & Bonawitz 2007), and social and emotional development (Dore, Smith, & Lillard 2015). One reason that play might be such a valuable pedagogical tool is that it features the precise contexts that facilitate learning. A research field called the *science of learning* has identified four key ingredients of successful learning: Learning occurs best when children are *mentally active* (not passive), *engaged* (not distracted), *socially interactive* (with peers or adults), and building *meaningful connections* to their lives (Hirsh-Pasek et al. 2015). These features are evident in play situations, including the one in Ms. Elena's classroom:

> Javon is mentally active when he thinks about where he learned the name of the place where chickens sleep and then uses the word *coop* appropriately. Sara is engaged when she chooses to be the cow and moves in concert with Javon and Ashish instead of being distracted by other groups at play. Ms. Elena made the word *coop* more meaningful for the children by making a connection to the children's visit to Maple Farm. Finally, the children were socially interactive when they built a play scenario that involved all three of them, with Ms. Elena joining in as a scaffolder.

These types of playful interactions between children and adults may be essential for supporting healthy social and emotional development. Guided play in particular features this type of social interaction and may lead to promising outcomes for learning and development.

What Is Guided Play?

Most researchers agree that play is fun, flexible, voluntary, and intrinsically motivated; it involves active engagement and often incorporates make-believe (Fisher et al. 2010; Lillard et al. 2013; Pellegrini 2009; Sutton-Smith 2001). Guided play maintains the joyful child-directed aspects of free play but adds an additional focus on learning goals through light adult scaffolding (Weisberg et al. 2016). It offers an opportunity for exploration in a context specifically designed to foster a learning goal. As such, it features two crucial elements: child agency (the child directs the learning) and gentle adult guidance to ensure that the child progresses toward the learning goal. Research suggests that guided play is a successful pedagogical tool for educators in a variety of areas (Weisberg et al. 2016). This chapter describes some examples of how preschool teachers can use guided play in the classroom to build specific language, mathematics, and spatial skills.

Language Development

Guided play is a model setting for language learning. For example, infusing vocabulary instruction in guided play fosters word learning for all preschoolers (Han et al. 2010; Toub et al. 2018). One study tested the effectiveness of word learning through guided play against a more teacher-directed learning activity (Toub et al. 2018). All children participated in shared book reading and then reviewed half of the vocabulary words through guided play and the other half through a picture card word-recall activity. The guided play resembled the learning taking place in the opening vignette. After play-based word learning, children defined the target words more readily than they did after picture card–based word learning.

Mathematics and Spatial Skills

Guided play is also effective for fostering spatial skills, which are important in and of themselves and are also tied to later mathematics success (Verdine et al. 2017). For example, a study with preschoolers (Fisher et al. 2013) compared children's ability to learn about geometry and shapes through guided play, free play, and direct instruction. In the guided play condition, the adult followed the children's lead and scaffolded the interaction. Children in this group learned more about geometry and shapes than those who participated in either the direct instruction condition, where the children listened passively while the adult delivered the content in an enjoyable way, or the free play condition, where children interacted with the shapes in whatever way they wished.

Guided play allows teachers to piggyback on children's joy and engagement to reinforce important skills.

To envision how a similar effect might occur in the classroom, imagine a different center in Ms. Elena's room:

> Pablo, Keisha, and Nari arrive at a table filled with tiles of different shapes. They all pick up pieces and begin snapping Magna-Tiles together. Nari says, "I'm going to build a tower! I can't get these pieces to fit." Ms. Elena is observing the children and chooses this moment to join in and say, "What shapes do you have, Nari?" Pablo says, "Nari has a square." "That's right, Pablo. Nari has a square. Nari, can you find another square?" Nari holds up a square. Ms. Elena says, "What makes that a square?" She pauses to let the children think about it, then continues, "It has four sides that are all the same length." She then says, "I wonder if it's possible to make a bigger square using the pieces you are holding up." Keisha says, "Hmm . . . I want to try!" The children look at each other and lay the pieces down—eventually discovering that by putting all four of the squares together, they create a larger square. Ms. Elena notices their discovery, and says, "Wow! You made a bigger square! It still has four sides, and all of the sides are the same length. Perhaps you can use this square as part of the tower you want to build, Nari."

Ms. Elena wove the definition of a square into the children's play, and she also encouraged the children to push themselves to make an important discovery about the shape tiles. Guided play allows teachers to piggyback on children's joy and engagement to reinforce important skills.

Why Does Guided Play Foster Learning? Fledgling Evidence from Brain Science

Guided play represents an *enhanced discovery* approach to learning that increases children's knowledge through opportunities to receive immediate, meaningful adult feedback (Alfieri et al. 2011). It is also an ideal example of an active, engaged, meaningful, and socially interactive learning context (Hirsh-Pasek et al. 2015). Consider, for instance, children playing with a shape sorter that lights up under certain conditions. The children discuss how to insert the shapes so that the sorter lights up. They keep inserting shapes and notice that sometimes the sorter lights up and sometimes it doesn't, but they can't figure out why. Their teacher joins in and makes some gentle guiding suggestions to help them by asking what the children have already tried and what they could try next. As children incorporate this feedback while continuing to experiment, they generate hypotheses and draw causal connections, becoming young scientists. Play helps children discover causal relationships through this type of informal experimentation (Gopnik 2012; Schulz & Bonawitz 2007). And light scaffolding, when needed, prevents frustration and enables children to engage in longer periods of playful experimentation.

Child-Guided and Adult-Guided Play and Learning Experiences

· ·

Developmentally appropriate practice provides purposeful, teacher-guided support balanced with responsiveness to children's choices and their self-directed initiation. The following principles describe some situations in which teachers might choose to support children as they initiate their own play experiences and some in which they provide more direct scaffolding and guidance.

Intentional teachers support child-guided learning experiences when children are

> Exploring materials, actions, and ideas actively and making connections on their own

> Establishing interpersonal relationships and learning from one another

> Considering and investigating their own questions about materials, events, and ideas

> Motivated to solve problems on their own

> So focused on their enterprise that adult intervention would be an interruption

> Challenging themselves and one another to master new skills

> Applying and extending existing knowledge and skills in new ways

These behaviors and attitudes signal to teachers that child-guided experience will be particularly fruitful, but this does not exclude using other teaching strategies and planned activities. Even when teachers pick up on cues like these, they will want to make strategic use of adult-guided experience to optimize children's learning.

Intentional teachers employ adult-guided learning experiences to

> Introduce children to a new material or experience

> Help children learn established systems of knowledge (such as letter names and number operations)

> Draw children's attention to something likely to interest them

> Encourage children to reflect on how or why something has happened, or consider what might happen "if . . ."

> Engage children with a skill or concept teachers know they will need for further learning

> Offer support and suggestions when children appear stalled, discouraged, or frustrated

> Scaffold experiences when children seem ready for the next level of mastery but may need assistance to attain it on their own

> Introduce a material or idea to a child who uses materials or actions repetitively over time

Although these behaviors and attitudes suggest that children will benefit from adult-guided learning experience, intentional teachers keep in mind that child-guided experience is an important part of the full learning picture.

Adapted from A.S. Epstein, *The Intentional Teacher: Choosing the Best Strategies for Young Children's Learning*, rev. ed. (Washington, DC: NAEYC, 2014), 238–39.

Adult-scaffolded play experiences might be particularly important because they help children develop what scientists call *proactive control:* neural mechanisms in the brain's prefrontal cortex that use clues from the environment to help the brain figure out what might happen next (Weisberg et al. 2014). Guided play might support the development of proactive control by fostering a *mise en place*—a term derived from the culinary world meaning "everything in its place" and suggested by the famed psychology professor Jerome Bruner (2013, personal communication with Brenna Hassinger-Das):

> Think about preparing to make a pizza. You gather the dough, sauce, cheese, and toppings. You also get out the required tools: rolling pin, pizza stone, and pizza cutter. In this way, you have prepared yourself and your workspace for the task at hand.

Similarly, a psychological *mise en place*—a readiness to anticipate events and explore an activity (Weisberg et al. 2014)—helps children prepare their minds to embrace learning experiences in a positive way. Ms. Elena cultivated such a *mise en place* through her inclusion of farm-focused play activities. By preparing the play environment for the children to learn the focus words, Ms. Elena enabled them to work toward this goal in their own playful way. This type of gently scaffolded, playful learning fosters children's desire to seek out similar meaningful learning opportunities (Weisberg et al. 2014).

Imagine a different week in Ms. Elena's classroom. Drawing on an interest that several children have shown recently, she sets up one center with a castle play set that mirrors a book read during that week's storybook theme of knights and dragons. The prepared play set encourages children's organic use of the theme's vocabulary words as they play—words like *talons* and *nostrils*. Ms. Elena can then draw attention to these words and help children make meaningful connections to them. This type of adult support during guided play may be the mechanism through which children's fledgling proactive control mechanisms emerge (Weisberg et al. 2014).

Looking Forward

The bottom line is that play is ubiquitous across species, and it likely has a significant role in many aspects of human development. Though behavioral research is still unfolding (Lillard et al. 2013; for a rebuttal, see Weisberg et al.

2013), evidence is mounting that guided play scaffolds young children's development and that it might prime critical neural mechanisms to help children anticipate how to respond to learning moments (Weisberg et al. 2014). It also helps children develop an understanding of how the world works (Gopnik 2012). To deepen our understanding, research investigating play's biological foundation in children is urgently needed. This research would provide a critical foundation for supporting calls to increase opportunities for play in all early childhood classrooms and to promote playful home environments.

As we await new discoveries from brain science, one finding is already clear: Play is a wonderful context for active, engaged, meaningful, and socially interactive learning. And, as two of the authors of this piece describe in their book *Becoming Brilliant: What Science Tells Us About Raising Successful Children,* play also prepares children to become social, caring, thinking, and creative citizens (Golinkoff & Hirsh-Pasek 2016). In fact, many researchers and teachers now concur that the "child-driven educational methods sometimes referred to as 'playful learning' are the most positive means yet known to help young children's development" (Lillard et al. 2013, 28).

Try This!

> Consider how you can introduce new vocabulary words that are relevant to the context of the children's play. For example, if children are pretending to move chickens to the barn, explain that a henhouse is called a coop. Solicit their ideas about the similarities and differences between a coop and a barn.

> Add specific information to what children say. For example, when a child says, "It's a barn," you can respond, "Yes, a barn is a building where animals live. The farmer stores food in the loft." While looking at a bird feeder together, you might say, "That red bird is a cardinal. It pokes its beak into the seeds."

> As children act out their dramatic play scenes, notice how they use props and what they say. What skills are emerging? What additional props could you add to help them try out new skills or refine their play strategies?

> Provide open-ended props (e.g., boxes, sponges, gloves, containers, tubes) and items that add complexity to play themes (e.g., clipboards for menus, play money for a store). As children begin to build and play, ask what props they need for their castle, boat, store, or house. They will surprise you with your insights and ideas.

naeyc ®
Accreditation
Early Learning Programs

This chapter supports the following NAEYC Early Learning Program Accreditation Standards and topic areas:

Standard 2: Curriculum
2.B Social and Emotional Development
2.D Language Development
2.F Early Mathematics

Standard 3: Teaching
3.E Responding to Children's Interests and Needs
3.F Making Learning Meaningful for All Children

The author of this chapter describes teachers in playful learning environments as "subtle participants and gentle guides," sparking children's curiosity about concepts in ways that make them want to learn more. Yet she also openly shares her ongoing concern about ensuring that children are indeed learning skills and knowledge through play. You may feel the same way. As you read, consider your own thoughts and perhaps reservations about a more child-centered approach to teaching. Does the information shared by the author reaffirm your belief in and commitment to developmentally appropriate practice? What can you learn about achieving a balance of child-directed and teacher-guided learning in your program?

2

Observing, Planning, Guiding: How an Intentional Teacher Meets Standards Through Play

Patricia McDonald

It is early in the day. Kris, one of my 22 kindergartners, is sharing her journal entry and drawing with me. After our talk, she walks to the carpet to play. She observes a group of children who have discovered that the magnifying glasses we used during this morning's math lesson enlarge words found throughout the room. She then joins a group that is building a house out of blocks, carefully balancing different shapes on top of each other. After about 30 minutes, I announce it's time for morning meeting. The class responds with, "Awwww! Can't we keep playing?"

When I taught kindergarten, I strove to provide an engaging environment where play was the prominent support for and means of learning. But in truth, I found it challenging. Early in my career I used a didactic approach full of worksheets and drills because it was expected. While I see small amounts of direct instruction as useful, I also know that play-based learning is essential for young children. Play encompasses knowledge building, problem solving, communicating, and collaborating; yet throughout my career I often felt that the field was gently nudging me toward focusing on "skills and drills." Even after 23 years as a teacher, I felt torn between ensuring the children achieved certain benchmarks at certain times and offering a more child-centered education that created opportunities for exploration.

The current educational emphasis on standards and high-stakes assessments places tremendous pressure on teachers and children, leading to "potentially problematic teaching practices" (NAEYC 2009, 4). Considering the long lists of specific objectives that must be accomplished by the end of the year—usually without extended learning time or other additional resources—it is easy to understand why teachers would be skeptical about devoting their limited class time to child-centered approaches to instruction. Child-directed, playful learning is often less efficient than teacher-directed learning, but if we value healthy child development, we must find a balance in our classrooms (see Hassinger-Das, Hirsh-Pasek, & Golinkoff, this volume).

The Teacher's Role

Anna and Lizzy are buying items at the "grocery market," a project the children initiated and constructed after a lesson on community. They had sorted grocery items, made signs advertising discounts, and set up a checkout area with bags and play money. I see an opportunity to introduce money. I walk over to Carly, the cashier, and ask, "How much are the grapes?" "Ten cents," she replies. I hold out a handful of coins and say, "Can you help me? What coins do I need for 10 cents?" Anna says, "Look for the one that says 10 cents." "Where do you see that?" Lizzy asks. "It's really small," I reply. "Let's get the magnifying glass to see it."

Later, we have a class discussion about the names of the coins and their characteristics, using magnifying glasses as tools. After our conversation, the coins and magnifying glasses are put in the exploration center, where the children quickly learn that they can magnify other objects, including print.

When children play, teachers are researchers, observing children to decide how to extend their learning both in the moment and by planning new play environments. They must figure out how to quietly intervene to help children connect contexts to everyday concepts and academic content in a way that supports each child's strengths and needs, leading to further cognitive, social, and emotional development (Fleer 2009; NAEYC & NCTM [2002] 2010). By strategically expanding play and asking questions that challenge children's thinking, teachers create meaningful learning opportunities to help children develop a deeper understanding based on their observations, ideas, and judgments (Blake 2009). A mix of child-directed and guided play, in which the teacher expands on the play experience with questions or suggestions, should be incorporated into the day. When the play environment is intentionally created, the learning that occurs is as deliberate and logical as in any teacher-directed lesson, yet the activities are offered in a manner that is appropriate to the development of each child (Leong & Bodrova 2012).

In my classroom, children played every day, but I was never "just letting children play." I was observing, guiding, and planning.

> I watch with curiosity as David and Marco grab a stack of playing cards. They look tentatively at each other, then turn to me, saying, "We're not sure what to play." I show them a card game in which they will practice cooperation and further develop their number sense. I explain the need for a "caller" who distributes the cards and directs the other players when to flip over their top card. The player holding the card with the highest numerical value wins that round.
>
> Anna walks over and watches. "Would you like to play?" I ask. She smiles and joins in. After we play another round, I excuse myself from the game; the players all agree to vote on who will take my place as the caller. Anna is chosen, but it isn't long before I observe Marco throwing his cards on the floor, frustrated that Anna is telling him what to do. I remind the group about their vote, and they continue playing.
>
> Later, when another child joins in, the same problem arises—but the children don't need my help. Marco explains that one person needs to be the caller.

When children play, teachers are researchers, observing children to decide how to extend their learning both in the moment and by planning new play environments.

This situation reflected my many roles as a teacher (Synodi 2010). In the beginning, I was an *observer,* expecting (based on prior observations) that the two boys would likely need some help initiating play. As an *instructional leader,* I selected a game that would develop their academic and social abilities. As a *participant,* I modeled a new game and invited another child to join the group. When the first dispute occurred, I became the *mediator,* emphasizing the agreed-on rules.

During play-based learning, teachers are often subtle participants or gentle guides who seek to enrich or expand on the present experience. With the card game, I was able to reinforce an important math concept (comparing number values) and support the children's growing abilities to work with others and regulate their feelings.

In this case, setting time aside for play resulted in a teachable moment when David and Marco asked for my help—but such opportunities do not always occur. As a teacher dedicated to providing significant amounts of playtime every day, I continually asked myself: How can I extend the play experience that I'm watching to connect it to the standards I'm required to teach? Knowing the standards is a preface to making this happen, as was the case with the grocery store. Realizing that the Common Core Mathematics Standards for kindergarten assert that children will write numbers from 0 to 20 (K.CC.A.3) as well as connect counting to cardinality (K.CC.B.4), creating a grocery store encouraged the children to engage with these specific standards. Writing out price tags, counting pieces of fruit, and describing the exchange of objects using quantities and numbers all supported meaningful ways to learn math.

From Theory to Reality

Some may argue that play is an inappropriate means of achieving standards. I have found that children can meet and exceed standards through playful learning that combines open-ended experiences, child-directed initiatives, and teacher-guided activities. However, as simple as play may sound, I will admit that achieving a balance between accomplishing set curricular goals and sustaining a child-centered environment is more difficult than one would think (Ranz-Smith 2007). Through experience, I learned that there were three primary factors I needed to address to bring play and standards together: being intentional in crafting activities, identifying children's developmental needs, and assessing growth.

Intentionally Crafting Activities

To address specific academic standards, I sometimes introduced a concept with a whole-group activity, then established an environment that supported further exploration during free-play time. I consciously determined the purpose and intentionality of all activities (including play), asking myself, "Do all of the materials and activities have a purpose that

supports what children need and understand?" It is the meaningfulness of the activities, as determined by the child, that creates a springboard for learning through curiosity and exploration (NAEYC & NAECS/SDE 2003).

An example of my effort to use play as a primary means of learning is a lesson in which I introduced the concept of sinking and floating. We were learning about life in the ocean at that time, which prompted a child-directed discussion about boats and why they are able to float in the water. I engaged the children in making boats out of foil and seeing how many coins it took to sink their boats. I introduced the idea that density and shape, not size, determine whether an object floats. After giving a demonstration to the whole group, I made the activity an independent center for the children to explore. I watched as they eagerly tried to make boats, which was quickly followed by piling up coins and revising their boat designs. While the beginning of the activity was a group demonstration, it motivated the children to explore their own questions independently and to investigate and challenge their assumptions.

I am certain that the children enjoyed, and learned a great deal from, this activity—but was this an example of play? If play must be open ended, child selected, and voluntary, play did not happen until after my demonstration. However, the demonstration sparked the children's curiosity and provided some basic concepts to start investigating; by having the time, space, and materials to further explore and experiment on their own, they engaged with science and engineering standards (such as making observations, gathering information, and developing a tool) and tried out their ideas through a playful experience. As a result, the children acquired new knowledge about developing and designing potential solutions. This allowed me to create more intentional plans for future learning.

Play is beneficial because it allows for more variation than many teacher-directed lessons.

Identifying Developmental Needs

One of the greatest yet most challenging facets of teaching kindergarten is accepting that individual development has its own time frame. To honor individual development, teachers do their best to implement activities that are suitable for each child. Play is beneficial because it allows for more variation than many teacher-directed lessons. With children varying in their current abilities and needs cognitively, socially, emotionally, and physically, having a flexible approach to teaching and learning—including lots of time for free and guided play—is essential. An illustration of how I applied this understanding involved the changes I made to my classroom schedule so the children could continue to try out and refine their new puzzle-solving strategies.

> Four children walk over to a puzzle on a table. They try to put the pieces together through random trial and error. Seeing that they have no strategy with which to solve the puzzle, I initiate a conversation on how to use the shapes of the lines to connect pieces and how to look for key images to determine the overall picture. Ten minutes later the timer rings to clean up. "But we didn't finish!" they tell me. Realizing the high-quality learning they were engaged in while playing with the puzzle (an activity that the children chose), I tell them we will have more time later in the day to finish. At lunch, I rearrange the daily schedule to offer more time for intentional choices and flexibility rather than defined and required work.

Knowing that a developmentally appropriate environment does not mean giving the children full control of the classroom, I focused on designing choices that were active and engaging. For example, I incorporated math games (including board and card games) into our morning meeting and restructured recess to allow more time for outdoor exploration (including science investigations). Materials (such as paint, tape, and musical instruments) that I had previously brought out only on special occasions, I made available for the children to use during open play every day. Sometimes my observation of the children led to a more individualized modification of routines, such as allowing a few minutes of individual quiet time to read or play for the child who did not prefer to participate in group work. For a child who appeared overwhelmed with choices, I might provide more specific toys and materials based on that child's interests.

Assessing Growth

Overall, my instructional approach was based on my knowledge of children's development and effective teaching practices. However, the direction of learning and specific activities were determined by my ongoing observation of the children's interests, abilities, and efforts. For me, assessment included seeking evidence of children's learning and honestly reflecting

on my own practice. I regularly asked myself whether I had an effective instructional plan in place and, if so, what I could expect the children's growth to look like.

In kindergarten, teachers use a variety of evaluation tools, such as portfolios, running records, anecdotal notes and narratives, and formal assessments that measure acquisition and application of skills and concepts. As I shifted toward play-based learning and created more time for child-directed activities, I carefully observed children's interests, efforts, and growth. Over time, I found that the combination of observing play and conducting skill-specific assessments provided well-balanced information. Examining both, I was able to determine the direction of learning and develop activities that were appropriate, flexible, and challenging, including more free and guided play.

Reflection

In my experience, there were times when trying to make the academic standards meaningful while guiding and extending children's interests and curiosity felt like a walk in the dark. In putting aside the safety of worksheets and trusting in the guidance provided by the children, I found myself wondering on a daily basis, What did the children gain today from being in my class? Did I miss an opportunity for learning? Did I reinforce the connection between

Play provides experiences that contribute to children's present knowledge and abilities that they will rely on when solving problems in the future.

intentionality, developmentally appropriate activities, and assessment? Based on my observation, what did they learn from playing? While my answers were almost always much richer than they were when I relied heavily on worksheets, I found that these questions were essential to my ever-increasing intentionality, and thus to the children's learning.

Although children may not fully understand the broader ideas they are exploring while playing, play provides experiences that contribute to their present knowledge and abilities that they will rely on when solving problems in the future (NAEYC & NCTM [2002] 2010). Teachers' professional knowledge of child development and of individual children's abilities, needs, and cultural backgrounds directly impacts instruction and the creation of an effective play-based learning environment (NAEYC 2009). When teachers connect academic standards to play activities, they free themselves to support the overall development of children.

Try This!

As you prepare materials for children to explore and observe how children respond to them, ask yourself the following questions:

› What specific purpose does each material serve?

› What do you see children doing, talking about, comparing, and trying out? What does this tell you about what they might be thinking?

› What opportunities do you see to add complexity, introduce vocabulary, or prompt higher-level thinking?

› Think about ways to reinforce connections between the purpose of materials and activities, what children know and can do, active engagement, and age-appropriate assessment tools.

› Notice how children respond to your gentle prompting and guiding. How do you see their engagement with materials and play partners change as you offer suggestions and guidance?

Accreditation

Early Learning Programs

This chapter supports the following NAEYC Early Learning Program Accreditation Standards and topic areas:

Standard 2: Curriculum
2.A Essential Characteristics

Standard 3: Teaching
3.E Responding to Children's Interests and Needs
3.F Making Learning Meaningful for All Children
3.G Using Instruction to Deepen Children's Understanding and Build Their Skills and Knowledge

Standard 4: Assessment
4.C Identifying Children's Interests and Needs and Describing Children's Progress
4.D Adapting Curriculum, Individualizing Teaching, and Informing Program Development

PART TWO

Providing Rich Content Experiences Through Play

Playful learning can occur anywhere—but perhaps no other setting offers richer opportunities for children to connect learning to their daily lives and build on what they already know than the dramatic play area. It also offers abundant possibilities for language development, particularly for dual language learners. What rich language practices and connections does this chapter suggest to you for the children in your own program? Use what you know and learn about their cultures and experiences to provide culturally relevant dramatic play opportunities. What growth in children's language, socialization, initiative taking, and problem solving might you see as a result?

3

Supporting Language Through Culturally Rich Dramatic Play

**Irasema Salinas-Gonzalez,
María G. Arreguín-Anderson,
and Iliana Alanís**

For young children, play is the primary vehicle for learning about their environment, their culture, and other people. Play contributes to their social, emotional, and cognitive development, including their language, literacy, and brain development (Christie & Roskos 2009; Copple & Bredekamp 2009; Singer, Golinkoff, & Hirsh-Pasek 2006).

Traditionally, the dramatic play center is an area of the classroom generally set up as a "house corner" with a child-size stove, refrigerator, cupboard, table, and chairs. This is a place where young children draw from their resources and experiences to enhance their play. Because children use play representations and language to jointly create role-playing episodes, these interactions are often referred to as sociodramatic play (Selmi, Gallagher, & Mora-Flores 2015).

Children's sociodramatic play varies according to their unique cultural backgrounds, abilities, experiences, and languages. Culturally relevant play often occurs in sociodramatic spaces, which provide a natural context for interactions with other children who have varied proficiency levels in their home language and/or in their second language (Arreguín-Anderson, Salinas-González, & Alanís 2018). In these spaces, children reenact activities and observations from family life and share common events in their cultures, leading to meaningful learning—especially in language and vocabulary. Using children's *funds of knowledge*—the body of knowledge and competencies accumulated through their family and cultural experiences—teachers can create dramatic play centers that are grounded in children's cultural experiences (González, Moll, & Amanti 2005). This framework compels teachers to view children as important contributors to the planning and learning that takes place in the classroom.

In this chapter, we draw from a study that took place in a Spanish/English Head Start classroom in south Texas. We illustrate how the teacher, Mrs. Ramos, promoted conversations that led to the children generating themes for the classroom's dramatic play center that would provide enriching language experiences. Often, these types of conversations occurred during morning circle time, when she encouraged children to share their daily experiences. In one exchange, she asked her class of 17 emergent bilingual children to turn and talk to a partner about what they did over the weekend and then take turns sharing their experiences with the whole group.

> The children have noticed that *la paletería* (a food stand that sells frozen fruit Popsicles and ice cream treats), the most recent dramatic play center theme, has been taken down and put away, and they are wondering what kind of center should replace it.
>
> Mrs. Ramos invites them to talk about their weekend activities. Rodrigo says that he and his grandmother went to the *panadería* (bakery). Two children ask, "What is that?" Juanita explains,

"That's a bakery where you buy bread and cake." Mrs. Ramos says that she and her mother used to go to the panadería when she was a child, and this makes the children smile.

The conversation turns to *pan dulce* (sweet bread). Some children say they buy it at the local grocery store or corner store. Others say their families buy it at their nearby panadería. Mrs. Ramos suggests that this could be the theme of the new dramatic play center. The children enthusiastically begin naming baked goods that their panadería will sell, and Mrs. Ramos writes down their suggestions.

Culturally Responsive Centers

Like Mrs. Ramos, effective teachers can take advantage of opportunities to capture and interpret children's voices to re-create familiar themes, such as the local panadería, in their dramatic play center. Instead of setting up centers with themes that are isolated from children's life experiences, observant teachers create play opportunities that reflect the children's social worlds. As Mrs. Ramos did, teachers can draw on children's funds of knowledge and identify culturally relevant themes by listening to children talk in the classroom, on the playground, or at mealtime. What do they talk about? What do they draw or write about? What are their family life experiences and customs? Teachers use these real-life experiences as a basis for developing rich communication environments where children can develop their language and literacy skills. In the safe environment of culturally relevant play, young dual language learners are more likely to try new things, use their second language more boldly, and feel successful.

Using Mrs. Ramos's classroom as an example, the following are three strategies for providing language-rich environments and scaffolding language development to help dual language learners (in this case, emergent Spanish/English bilinguals) develop communication skills and learn new concepts through play experiences that are sensitive to their local community context.

Spark Conversations Through Verbal Mapping

To expose children to new vocabulary, practice *verbal mapping*—that is, describe to children what they are doing (or what you are doing). Remember to use new vocabulary words in conversations over and over again in a meaningful context, because children need to hear and practice using unfamiliar words many times to truly understand them. Describe actions and objects that are important to children while in a familiar and meaningful setting, such as a bodega, a paletería, or a panadería.

Children's sociodramatic play varies according to their unique cultural backgrounds, abilities, experiences, and languages.

Jorge explains that in his neighborhood bakery, people use *pinzas para pan,* or tongs, to pick up bread. Mrs. Ramos sees this as an opportunity to reinforce the word *tongs.* She hands Jorge two wooden blocks and says, "Good morning, sir. I'm delivering the two tongs the manager ordered for the bakery." Although *tongs* is a new word for the children, they immediately integrate it into their speech and play. The cashier tells the next customer, "Please give me your tray so I can ring up your bread. Leave the tongs over there."

Mrs. Ramos also engages in verbal mapping by talking about the types of bread customers buy. Without disrupting the children's play, Mrs. Ramos asks questions, supplies vocabulary, and extends the conversation to support their language development.

Provide New Props to Extend Children's Play

Add props to the dramatic play center in phases to build on children's knowledge and extend their interest. Try placing new props in the center for children to discover, then explain how to use them. Or you might introduce the new props through role-playing, as Mrs. Ramos did with the tongs. Here's how she set up the panadería (see also "Prop Suggestions for the Panadería").

Phase 1

Provide basic props related to the play theme. Offer—or invite families to contribute—common objects and tools, such as photos/pictures of familiar breads, aprons, spice and extract bottles, plastic mixing bowls, wooden spoons, rolling pins, and other kitchen products or tools.

Phase 2

Add more props based on careful observation of children's interactions. After Mrs. Ramos observed children talking about delivering cakes for weddings and *quinceañeras* (girls' 15th birthday celebrations), she introduced a calendar. The children marked the dates when cakes had to be delivered to or would be picked up by customers. Other items provided included cookie cutters and a receipt booklet.

Phase 3

Add props that enhance the theme. One day Mrs. Ramos placed a pretend fire extinguisher in the bakery. This extended children's imaginations (and vocabulary) as they role-played burning bread and putting out a fire. She also supplied objects like a bakery timer, cake photo album, and pictures of celebrations.

Prop Suggestions for the Panadería

Phase 1: Initial Props

- aprons
- baker's hats
- baking trays/cookie sheets
- bowls
- cash register
- containers (for sugar and flour)
- extract bottles
- measuring cups
- oven (cardboard box)
- oven mitts
- paper bags
- paper and pens
- plastic gloves
- playdough
- pretend bread or photos of bread
- rolling pin
- spice bottles
- variety of paper and writing tools
- wallet

Phase 2: Props added after teachers' systematic observation

- appointment book
- bread boxes
- bulletin board
- *cajeta* (caramel sauce)
- calendar
- coffee container
- coffeepot
- cookie cutters
- dry-erase board
- hairnet
- open/closed sign
- *piloncillo* (unrefined brown sugar)
- receipt booklet
- tongs
- tortilla press

Phase 3: Props deliberately added to enhance interest and imagination

- bakery delivery van
- bakery on wheels
- baking timer
- cake photo album
- cell phone
- pretend fire extinguisher
- pictures of celebrations
- pictures of community
- quinceañera birthday dress

This dramatic play center reflected the Spanish-speaking children in the class. But classes have all sorts of cultural mixes. Regularly assess the materials and props in the dramatic play center to make sure they accurately reflect all of the children and families in your class and accommodate children with disabilities. Add props that encourage children to talk to each other and to you. When the excitement over a certain dramatic play center fades, offer new props or change the theme.

Make It a Print-Rich Setting

Create a welcoming, print-rich dramatic play center. Add functional labels, pictures, books, and other materials reflective of children's cultures, such as familiar recipes, photos of cultural sweet breads, and spice or extract bottles (for example, vanilla, cinnamon, or *piloncillo*—unrefined brown sugar). Mrs. Ramos labeled the panadería shelves with the names of different breads and other baked goods that children had heard their families talk about, such as *empanadas*, *conchas*, and *orejas*. Seeing how these words are spelled encouraged the children to write the words as they were ordering or selling sweet bread or creating new bread recipes.

An interesting space encourages children to stay engaged. Children notice the print and learn that it symbolizes language. Using the props, they learn the everyday functions of writing and literacy. When Mrs. Ramos placed an Open/*Abierto* sign on the panadería counter, some children said, *"Ya está abierta la panadería!"* ("The bakery is open!")

Place useful labels to help children organize the materials. Also have labels the children can touch and even copy and trace. Mrs. Ramos made labels in Spanish and English for the names and prices of specific baked goods. The Open/*Abierto* sign and the different labels helped children organize their thought process as they created sequenced role-playing episodes. The labels also worked as resources to scaffold the children's oral language and assist with reading.

Facilitating Children's Play

Be aware of the significance of your role as facilitator of productive sociodramatic play. When you intentionally create interesting experiences for children that build on what they already know and are familiar with, their play becomes deeper and more interactive. Since play and language are mutually reinforcing, deepening the complexity of children's play potentially benefits their language development. But the support you provide during dramatic play has to be intentionally planned to assist young children to reach more mature levels of play (Leong & Bodrova 2012). Guide children's play based on your observations and on your knowledge of their individual needs. Sometimes children's play mainly involves simple role-playing scripts, with minimal interaction with their peers, and the children may need help socializing with others during their play. Sometimes their play becomes repetitious, and you might intervene to offer a new idea that encourages children to extend their play theme (Sluss 2015) or one that challenges the children's current thinking and roles.

Your intervention is most responsive and effective when it remains true to the children's intent. Mrs. Ramos used a nonintrusive approach as she asked thoughtful questions related to the play she observed, supplied vocabulary, and extended the sociodramatic play conversations. For example, in the panadería she reminded children to write down the bread orders and to mark down their calendars when they had a delivery to make. She intentionally labeled the shelf displaying the various types of breads and provided writing materials.

Mrs. Ramos also modeled communication and play behaviors by occasionally participating in the dramatic play center with children. On one occasion she noticed Jorge throwing "bread" (paper cutouts) on the floor while Carlos laughed. Mrs. Ramos entered the play by pretending to be a concerned customer who noticed the bread on the floor. She approached Alberto, the baker, and said, "Good afternoon! I want to buy five conchas, but there are no more left on the shelf. They are on the floor! Let's call a custodian to help clean it up." Alberto agreed and asked the other boys to help, which they agreed to do.

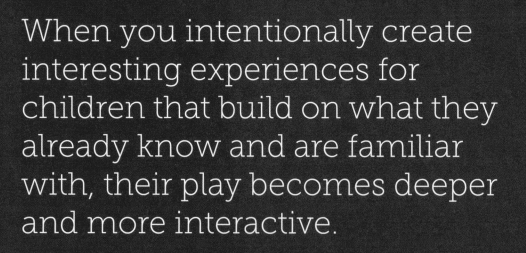

When you intentionally create interesting experiences for children that build on what they already know and are familiar with, their play becomes deeper and more interactive.

Conclusion

Children's language development is enhanced by intentional support from teachers, interaction with peers during play, and meaningful opportunities to practice their new communication skills. Center themes encourage children to collaborate and talk about what is personally meaningful to them, enabling them to enjoy new words in a safe, comfortable setting. Including familiar objects, props, open-ended materials, and literacy resources in the dramatic play center provides opportunities for language that the children already understand as they are acquiring new language labels. These materials create a sense of connection that is fundamental in children's development of cultural identity and language learning. As children practice representing things, experiences, and people through their play, this will eventually help them to represent their ideas with letters and words (Christie & Roskos 2009).

We hope our examples inspire you to create dramatic play centers that reflect the children's communities, cultures, and experiences outside of school.

Try This!

› Listen to children's everyday talk to learn about the places they visit, the activities they enjoy, and the people who are part of their daily life adventures. In response, make a list of themes, current vocabulary words, and additional vocabulary that expands on children's experiences, knowledge, and ideas.

› Explore your dramatic play area. Does it reflect all children's cultural backgrounds and abilities? Are objects labeled in their home languages and in English? Are basic props unusual, interesting, or engaging? Are materials labeled and organized for ease of use? What signs could be added to highlight the play theme (e.g., bakery, market, fire station, street sign)?

› Create a Phase 1, 2, and 3 chart for your dramatic play area as the authors suggest. Follow the sequence to add initial props, enhanced materials in response to your systematic observation, and props added deliberately to promote interest and imagination.

naeyc® Accreditation

Early Learning Programs

This chapter supports the following NAEYC Early Learning Program Accreditation Standards and topic areas:

Standard 2: Curriculum
2.A Essential Characteristics
2.D Language Development

Standard 3: Teaching
3.A Designing Enriched Learning Environments
3.B Creating Caring Communities for Learning
3.F Making Learning Meaningful for All Children

Many times, playful learning occurs as children take off with an idea or concept you introduce and make it their own, leading to delightful, surprising discoveries and connections. As you read how exploration of a piece of fine art sparked the children's imaginations and creativity and led to their growth across many domains, think about the ways storytelling and acting encourage problem solving and critical thinking. While you may not always foresee the paths children's explorations will take, how can you respond as their ideas and actions unfold, and then embed learning in the experiences that result?

4

Connecting Art, Literacy, and Drama Through Storytelling

Bonnie Ripstein

"There's a story in my picture!" exclaims 5-year-old Andrew as he shows me the drawing he has been working on. Eager to document his comments, I quickly grab my recorder and ask him to tell me his story. After I transcribe his words, we share his picture and story with the class.

The Mystical Tree, by Andrew

Once upon a time, there was a little mystical tree and the sun always shined on it when there was sunlight. There was a family called the Leonards and they had a dog and they lived near the tree. So, the mystical tree had a crystal inside it and if anybody touched it or took it, the whole world would go away. Nobody ever touched it because the mystical tree is guarding it. The mystical tree never ever let anybody touch it, only see it, because that's the way it is. And the tree is old, about 150 years.

This was the first time I had seen Andrew excited about sharing his work. He was a creative artist and loved storytelling, but Andrew rarely revealed these strengths to his classmates because he struggled with English literacy, as Russian was his first language. Now, three months into the school year, he was opening up—and we were all benefiting from his creative spark.

I taught both preschool and kindergarten classes at the Henry Barnard Laboratory School, located on the campus of Rhode Island College, for 14 years. The school partners with the college's education department to provide its students in preschool through fifth grade with experienced faculty who also serve as instructors at the college. Faculty members are given the opportunity to explore varied approaches to teaching, and I had chosen to research and explore the Reggio Emilia approach.

As a Reggio follower, one of my goals was to integrate more visual arts into the curriculum. Reggio fosters children's intellectual development through a systematic focus on symbolic representation, including words, movement, drawing, painting, building, sculpture, shadow play, collage, dramatic play, and music (Edwards, Gandini, & Forman 1993). Loris Malaguzzi, founder of the Reggio Emilia approach, once said, "Our task, regarding creativity, is to help children climb their own mountains, as high as possible. No one can do more. Creativity seems to emerge from multiple experiences . . ." (Edwards, Gandini, & Forman 1998, 76–77).

With these thoughts in mind, I began the school year with a study of a painting by Miyuki Tanobe titled *Monday, Washing-Day* (*Lundi, jour de lessive,* 1972; see the image on page 47). This lively, detailed painting depicts an urban neighborhood in which young children are playing on a small, grassy spot in front of weathered apartment buildings under lines of laundry and a gray, cloudy sky. I chose this piece of art to explore with the children because it contained several elements they could relate to, such as familiar toys, colorful clothing, an outside environment, and a rainy day. In addition, I was aware that the children's art teacher began the school year by studying lines and shapes with the children.

As children look at works of art, they use their imaginations and prior knowledge to determine what is happening, why, and how they would feel if they were in the scene (Mulcahey 2009). When I first introduced *Monday, Washing-Day* to the children, I asked, "What do you see?" The children focused on the painting's colors, shapes, and objects.

Ellen: I saw a baby and little lines on her socks.

Harriet: I saw some flowers on her umbrella.

Singh: I saw underwear and socks.

Roberto: I noticed blue, orange, and white.

Colleen: The artist had bubbles. He put swirls of colors in them.

Grant: I see kind of like squiggly lines.

Harriet: He kind of did this. (*Paints in the air with her finger*). Kind of scribbly.

Monday, Washing-Day (Lundi, jour de lessive), 1972. Courtesy of Miyuki Tanobe

I acknowledged the children's comments and followed up with questions designed to elicit some sharing of their own experiences.

Over the next several months, as I periodically asked the children to reconsider the painting, they began to engage in more critical thinking—interpreting the feelings represented and the story being told by the artist. We spent approximately 10 to 15 minutes a week reviewing the painting. Each discussion began with a question to promote higher-level thinking. After starting with asking "What do you see?," I moved in subsequent sessions to "What do you notice?," "How does the painting make you feel?," and "What might be happening outside of the painting?" Each session began with a review of and reflection on what had been previously discussed.

Oren: Rainstorm is coming, dark clouds and no puddles. Maybe these are bad guys that put the clothes outside before it's going to rain. This sky is dark, no sun.

Alexandria: Maybe it was night and it rained and they got dirty and had to wash those clothes.

Grant: (*Looks at the boy in a purple shirt behind the fence.*) He sees a flatbed truck, but the flatbed truck has a big box on it. It's at nighttime and that is showing the light.

Harriet: It's raining at night and that's why it's bright. Maybe the people are wearing bright colors to make it look like the sun.

Colleen: It rained, it is dark, and there's an umbrella. But it is a picnic and the people are happy.

Madina: Happy. It might have rained after they were outside and they're having fun in the rain.

How to Choose Works of Art

When searching for artwork to share with young children, consider how a piece will engage them.

> Will the children relate to the environment depicted?

> What connections to children's prior knowledge, experiences, and families can you help children make?

> What opportunities might the work offer for children to use their imaginations or explore their feelings?

> What concepts from your curriculum can you connect to?

> Is there enough content in the artwork for it to be used in an extended exploration?

> What elements of diversity does the artwork incorporate?

Local and national art museums offer troves of art resources. Most of them have links for educators as well as for children. Here are two that I have found particularly helpful:

> The Metropolitan Museum of Art (www. metmuseum.org) has links to lesson plans and other resources for educators.

> The National Gallery of Art (www.nga.gov) has resources for educators and a site specifically for children (NGAKids).

Search online for other sources. Here is one that I found helpful:

> The Bird Feed NYC (www.thebirdfeednyc. com/2012/02/12/works-of-art-to-share-with-young-children) includes a selection of works of art for young children as well as questions to ask about each one.

As the school year progressed, I began to see ways that the children's thinking about the painting were expressed in other aspects of their day. In their dramatic play episodes, I heard comments such as "It's raining. We need to take the laundry down!" When I read stories to them, they would stop me on each page with questions regarding the illustrations and how they related to the story line. The children's desire to tell stories about their own artwork increased, and their drawings and paintings began including more details, colors, and lines. Bubbles and swirls became a focus for many of their works. I was excited to see the children expressing their ideas and emotions through oral language and artwork. They were relating their perceptions of their world through their artwork in an environment that accepted and supported their thoughts (Feeney, Moravcik, & Nolte 2019). I also knew that they were building a strong foundation for first grade and beyond. In the early years, creating drawings and talking about them provides a natural transition to writing (Horn & Giacobbe 2007).

"My Picture Has a Story Too!"

Andrew's story about the mystical tree generated excitement about storytelling through art. After hearing his story, many children informed me that their paintings and drawings could tell stories too. Kindergartners have so much to say, but they often struggle to get all of their words down on paper. The basic conventions of writing, as well as their fine motor development, prevent them from easily documenting all of their thoughts. Kindergartners tend to reduce their ideas to one or two sentences, often leaving out important details because the words are "too hard to write." I wanted to provide a way for children to share their ideas and inventiveness without feeling hindered by their still-developing writing skills.

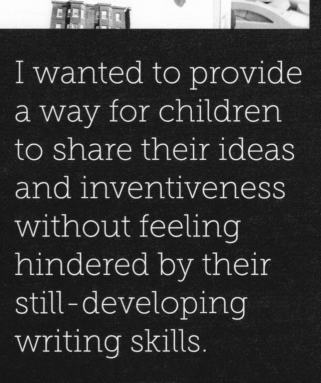

I wanted to provide a way for children to share their ideas and inventiveness without feeling hindered by their still-developing writing skills.

Building on our discussions of *Monday, Washing-Day,* in which we uncovered several possible stories behind the image, and drawing on Andrew's revealing of his story, I challenged the children to create their own artwork and then find *their* stories. I recorded each child's story using a video camera. The video was uploaded to a computer and then played back (in a one-on-one session with me) for the child to review or edit. The children were exposed to the processes of composing (in this case, thinking out loud or talking through their ideas) and revising, which are critical understandings and skills needed for learning to write (Schickedanz & Collins 2013). I then typed the story and once more reviewed it with the child for final approval. Once the children's stories and transcriptions were complete, they were shared with their peers using a document projector on a classroom screen.

Their finished products demonstrated their varying levels of understanding storytelling. Some children's work exhibited early knowledge of a beginning, middle, and ending, as well as the use of conflict and (perhaps to a lesser extent) resolution. Colleen's story, "Piece of Gold," for instance, packs all of these elements into a brief drama. "Swinging on the Sun," by Bruno, has more details but shows that Bruno is still developing his ability to craft a coherent and complete story.

Others described details in their drawings but had not yet mastered storytelling. Roberto's story, "The Treasure Box," for example, is not merely a description—he introduces the conflict of not being able to climb a box—but he seems to be wrapped up in the minutia and does not craft a beginning, middle, and end.

Bringing Their Stories to Life

Vivian Gussin Paley, an early childhood educator and researcher, designed a storytelling curriculum that encouraged language development and social interactions (1981). It was based on young children's need to act out their thoughts to further their understanding of the world around them. "The holistic nature of Paley's storytelling curriculum is evident in the learning it promotes in almost all areas of development, from using language to express and shape intention to making friends" (Cooper 2005, 230). Inspired by Paley, and looking to further the children's understanding of storytelling, I challenged them to act out the stories in their paintings. Some of the stories ended abruptly and lacked a true ending. I felt that if the children brought their stories to life, they might become more aware of story structure, with a beginning, middle, and ending. As young children often struggle with presentation skills, I also felt that providing them with a more personalized purpose would give them more confidence. Therefore, the writers became directors, choosing classmates to portray animals, people, and objects. They selected items from around the classroom to use as props.

As each child's turn came, we could see the excitement in their body language and facial expressions. For the children who struggled with writing, language, or social skills, it was their

Piece of Gold, by Colleen

The unicorn wanted to have a piece of gold. The leprechaun always came up with a bunch of tricks. One time he pretended he was on vacation but really hid behind a tree. The unicorn tried to take a piece of gold and the leprechaun took his tail.

Swinging on the Sun, by Bruno

There is a swing set on the sun and a meteor is crashing down on the earth. The person on the swing is saying "Run!" to the person on the ground. The person runs quickly and gets away, but the swing shakes and that person falls into the ocean. He swims back to the swing because the other people on the sun pushed a lever so the swing goes really low to the ocean. He swims to the swing and they push the lever and he goes back up.

The Treasure Box, by Roberto

There's a treasure box and the treasure box was shining. Someone wanted to climb the treasure box, but it was too bright and they fell down. There's another way to get down from the treasure box. Then you should go down here, no lines. It was from the old days, from the pirates and they dug a tunnel. Then you go and follow the path and go swimming with the fishes. If you are going down on the outside path and turn and roll down, you could fall into the shark swamp.

time to shine. Young children have wonderful ideas and thoughts in their heads, but when asked to put those thoughts down on paper, they become focused on the skills required to form the letters and words rather than on the content of their writing. Having the freedom to simply tell their stories provided more opportunities for creativity and interesting detail. The children who struggled with language and/or social skills were provided with support and encouragement throughout the project. Being chosen by their peers as actors gave them the confidence to play their part and to make their own choices later on. To these children, this was playtime. "Play is, in fact, a complex occupation, requiring practice in dialogue, exposition, detailed imagery, social engineering, literary allusion, and abstract thinking. Being both work and love for young children, play is absolutely essential for their health and welfare" (Paley 2009). And, I would add, exciting!

The joyful atmosphere that surrounded the room was infectious. It didn't matter if the stories were not completely coherent or lacked structure; supporting the development of the children's stories and providing them with the opportunity to share them with their peers in a new way gave their words significance. Many children read their stories as their peers performed in front of the remaining audience. Others asked me to read for them, with some choosing to perform in their own stories. I recorded their dramatics and then played the videos back to the entire class on the "big screen" the following day.

After we watched the videos, I asked the authors and their peers if they had any questions about the stories. The authors were excited and proud to answer these questions. The visual reflection and peer review helped the children see what was missing or needed to change so their stories would be clearer to everyone. Many authors added more details to their work based on their peers' feedback:

> Colleen included not only more characters but also a new ending. As the story was acted out, she realized that the unicorn and leprechaun didn't solve their problems—one lost a tail, the other the gold. Her revisions demonstrated an understanding of problem solution. As she explained, "I would put more trees around and a whole group of leprechauns. And more unicorns would come and they would all fight over the gold. In the end, a girl comes along and tells them to share the gold—and they do."

> For Bruno, his classmates' questions challenged his thinking, but he remained focused on details rather than on the story structure. The only revision Bruno made was adding a rocket to get to the sun. Many children asked him why there were people swinging on the sun; he simply replied, "Just because they are." When questioned about the crashing meteor problem, he said it was solved because the person on the swing saved the one on earth.

> After acting out his story, Roberto realized that it didn't have an ending—the boy was stuck in the swamp. To give his story clearer problems and solutions, as well as a beginning, middle, and ending, Roberto said, "I would change the fishes to piranhas and the sharks to sea monsters. The boy tries to get out of the swamp and he tosses a rock at the sea monster and climbs out. He tries one more time to get the treasure, but he slips and goes back home without any treasure."

Connecting Art, Literacy, and Drama

As I reflected on this project, I was amazed at how the introduction of a single fine art reproduction (and the activities that emerged as a result) fostered the children's developmental growth across many domains. I was particularly pleased to see the connections made between art, literacy, and drama. Through the exploration of *Monday, Washing-Day,* the children's observation skills and critical thinking improved. Their paintings and drawings began to demonstrate an understanding of the use of color, shape, and line to represent meaning. Their oral explanations of their paintings' stories gave significance to the children's work and allowed them to express their full ideas without having to worry about the conventions of getting their thoughts on paper. The children's dramatization of their stories brought their ideas to life and provided a stage for reflection, an introduction to peer review, and a meaningful opportunity for improving their stories. Directing, performing, and revising also promoted social confidence. Ultimately, a seemingly simple spark—Andrew's desire to tell his story—resulted in a combination of art, expression, and discussion that allowed all of the children to be successful in multiple ways.

Try This!

> Select an object of art, such as a drawing, painting, sculpture, collage, or mobile. Ask children, "What do you see?" Record their answers.

> When children draw or paint, consider asking them to express a story, idea, or experience that connects to their creation. Video-record and transcribe the children's stories.

> Provide time, space, and props for children to act out their stories. Ask children to describe what happened in the beginning, in the middle, and at the end of their stories.

> Encourage responses to child-created artwork and stories by asking the other children, "What do you see?" "What do you feel?" or "What do you want to know more about?"

naeyc®
Accreditation
Early Learning Programs

This chapter supports the following NAEYC Early Learning Program Accreditation Standards and topic areas:

Standard 1: Relationships
1.D Creating a Predictable, Consistent, and Harmonious Classroom

Standard 2: Curriculum
2.E Early Literacy
2.J Creative Expression and Appreciation for the Arts

Standard 3: Teaching
3.B Creating Caring Communities for Learning
3.E Responding to Children's Interests and Needs
3.F Making Learning Meaningful for All Children

As discussed in the introduction, playful learning might be an activity that the teacher initiates with children and for which she has specific learning goals in mind. In the situations described in this chapter, children eagerly engage in sorting shoes, playing card and board games, and creating shapes with rope and then determining the number of sides and angles—perhaps even without being aware that they're learning math concepts and skills. But the teachers have intentionally planned these activities to help children achieve not only math standards but also social skills in enjoyable, developmentally appropriate ways that provide for individualization. How does this chapter expand or challenge your idea of play and what playful instruction can look like?

5

Playful Math Instruction and Standards

Deborah Stipek

The children in Marylou's preschool class were wearing only one shoe when I walked in the door. I was confused. I expected to see a math lesson, and instead I saw children throwing their shoes into a pile. I soon understood, however, that this *was* a math activity.

Marylou has drawn a 6 x 10 grid on a shower curtain spread on the floor. She asks the children to sort the shoes into six piles, according to certain attributes they have agreed on—sandals, slip-ons, shoes with laces, etc. Then, in the bottom row of the grid, they place one shoe from each pile in its own square, followed by the rest of the shoes from that pile, one each in the squares above the first shoe. After the children count the number of shoes in each column, Marylou asks them what they notice, and the children discuss which categories have the most and the fewest shoes. She follows up with questions: Are there any categories that have the same number of shoes? How many more sandals than slip-ons are there?

Marylou replicates the grid on the chalkboard, and the children represent each shoe in each category with a letter (*L* for laces, etc.). Under each column, they write the total number of shoes in that category and continue the discussion: What kind of shoes did most children wear to school today? How many more Velcro shoes would they need for the Velcro column to be the same height as the slip-on column?

For the children, this activity was a game. For Marylou, it was serious business. In this one lesson she had the children engaged in multiple components of the math curriculum—categorization, basic number skills (counting, one-to-one correspondence, cardinality, writing numbers), graphing, and measurement.

In another preschool I visited, children explored the defining qualities of shapes. On the playground, three children stood in equally spaced positions with a rope pulled taut around them, forming an equilateral triangle. The teacher, Juan, asked them what shape they made and how many angles and sides there were. He then asked one of the children to move, keeping the rope taut, and repeated the questions. Juan also had children stand with a taut rope in groups of four, moving to create a rectangle with two long sides and two short sides, then moving to create four equal sides. He asked a series of questions: How many angles does the shape have? How many sides? What is a rectangle with equal sides called? What do all rectangles have in common? Some of the children who were not participating directly in the shape activity climbed a play structure to see the shapes from above, and they eagerly called out answers to Juan's questions.

In other classrooms, I have observed children enthusiastically count collections of erasers, small toy animals, colored cotton balls, and buttons, then represent their counts on paper—often by drawing the objects or a circle to represent each item and placing the objects on their representations to ensure an accurate count. I have watched young children play the card game War, counting the symbols (hearts, spades, clubs, diamonds) on each number card played to determine whose card has more. (Teachers can make the game more complex by having each child play two cards, add them, and then compare the sum with the other child's sum.) I have seen children hunt shapes in their classroom, debating whether a window with slightly curved corners is really a rectangle. I've witnessed a teacher read a picture book and ask children to find objects in front of, on top of, next to, and behind a house, and to identify the biggest and the smallest dogs in the illustrations.

Play Versus Academic Skills: It's Not a Zero-Sum Game

Did the children who were engaged in these activities know they were participating in math lessons? Probably not. But they were indeed learning math through what I refer to as *playful instruction.*

All of these activities were intentional on the part of the teacher, who had particular math learning goals in mind. All were carefully planned. All engaged children in active thinking, participating, and communicating. Some had the added value of allowing children to move around, making the activity more engaging for those who find it difficult to sit in one place. And in all of these activities, the teacher had an opportunity to assess children's understanding through observation and by inviting particular children to contribute to the conversation.

This may not look like standards-based academic teaching, but it is. Many teachers of young children are understandably anxious about standards and accountability pressures that have

These examples of playful math instruction make it clear that there is no need to choose between play and teaching academic knowledge and skills.

been pushed down to preschool. Many have shared with me concerns about how these pressures can interfere with what young children really need—daily opportunities to learn through play. Some teachers are also worried that teaching academic skills at an early age may undermine children's natural curiosity and motivation. But these examples of playful math instruction make it clear that there is no need to choose between play and teaching academic knowledge and skills. Abundant research has demonstrated that young children enjoy learning math and can learn far more than was previously assumed—without a single flashcard or worksheet (Carpenter et al. 2016; Clements & Sarama 2014; National Research Council 2001).

Playful math has an added bonus: Social skills development can easily be integrated into teacher-planned math activities. Research has shown that some types of board games (e.g., linear path games with lots of counting, like Chutes and Ladders) promote children's math abilities (Siegler & Ramani 2009). They also give children practice following rules, taking turns, and winning and losing gracefully. Similarly, children participating in Marylou's shoe categorization activity discussed and agreed on categories and raised their hands to answer questions, and everyone had a chance to participate. In Juan's shape activity, children negotiated who moved where in response to teacher directions and collaborated with others on the shape. In such situations, children are not learning math *instead* of social skills; they are learning math *and* social skills.

Teacher-Initiated Versus Child-Initiated Math Activities

Why are intentional, planned activities necessary? Don't teachers need to weave academic learning into activities initiated by children to make them child centered? For example, couldn't a teacher take advantage of children building a fort with blocks to help them learn about relative size? Couldn't she spontaneously offer a counting and comparison lesson to a group of children arguing about how many toy farm animals they each receive?

Yes, teachers can and should seize on naturally occurring learning opportunities as children play and explore. But there must be a balance. Relying entirely on spontaneous, child-initiated teachable moments would leave the order in which math concepts are introduced—or even *whether* they are introduced—too much to chance. Moreover, if teachers depend solely on child initiative, children's opportunities to learn will vary widely; some will have many opportunities, while others might have few. Playful instruction during planned small group and whole group activities provides systematic information about children's knowledge and skills, enabling teachers to keep track of what children understand and what support they need to grow and learn.

Making Standards, Accountability, and Packaged Curricula Work

Math standards do not preclude teachers implementing playful, engaging activities. And they can help teachers determine the content and order of the activities they develop. While accountability can be beneficial or problematic, depending on how it is implemented, math standards are still useful. They have been carefully crafted and vetted by diverse groups of content area experts and educators so teachers don't have to figure out everything on their own.

Standards can be intimidating, but they have value. The math standards developed in states, districts, and other organizations, such as Head Start, serve as a destination deemed desirable by experts. If teachers don't know where they want to end up, they will have a hard time figuring out how to get there.

Still, standards should guide, not dictate, instruction. I have observed some teachers who, anxious about meeting standards or following a standards-based curriculum, teach concepts that are too advanced for some children. When this happens, the children quickly become restless and frustrated—or just refuse to participate.

Adhering strictly to standards can also lead to underestimating what some children are ready to learn. A study of a nationally representative sample of kindergartners found that before they entered kindergarten, children had already mastered most of the mathematics skills kindergarten teachers reported teaching (Engel et al. 2016). For example, although the vast majority of children entered kindergarten having mastered basic counting and were able to recognize simple geometric shapes, their teachers reported spending about 13 days per month on this content. And although very few of the children entered kindergarten already knowing basic addition and subtraction, only about 9.5 days per month were devoted to those skills. The research further found that spending more time on content that was new to children, such as basic addition and subtraction, resulted in higher math achievement (Engel et al. 2016).

Ultimately, while standards help clarify annual learning goals, teachers must determine the short-term goals appropriate for their students. Children enter classes with varying knowledge and skills. Instruction needs to meet children where they are—or just a bit beyond where they are, in what the Russian psychologist Lev Vygotsky ([1930–35] 1978) refers to as the *zone of proximal development* (what a child can do with a little help or guidance). As children progress through preschool and the early elementary grades, some may need instruction focused on standards for children a year or two younger. They need to master those skills and that knowledge before they can tackle grade-level standards. This means that teachers need to adjust their instruction to help children master the prerequisite

Ultimately, while standards help clarify annual learning goals, teachers must determine the short-term goals appropriate for their students.

skills, and ideally schools need to provide some students with extra support. Other children may be ready to move on to developing the knowledge and skills expected of children one or even two years older. In brief, standards provide useful goalposts, but only the children themselves can show you where to start.

Road Maps Help

Knowing the final destination is a far cry from having a road map, which teachers also need for supporting children's progress. In addition to the standards, teachers need to know about the order in which children typically master math concepts and skills. By knowing typical learning trajectories, teachers can identify the next step in children's progression toward meeting a standard. And by understanding how their own students learn best, teachers can plan engaging, playful activities that help move children's thinking forward and respond to their individual strengths and needs.

Researchers now know a great deal about typical trajectories (e.g., see Clements & Sarama 2014). For example, when you add two objects to a set of six that a preschooler just counted and ask him how many are there now, most children will initially count the entire new set from the beginning (from one to six) before counting the last two. Later, at a more advanced level, they will "count on"—that is, start with the number of the previous set (six) and add the additional objects (seven, eight) to get the total (Siegler 2016). The child who starts again from the beginning needs help learning to remember the previous count. The teacher might play a "hide the set" game by putting her hand or a cup over the set and asking the child if she can figure out how many there are without seeing the items she already counted. The child who counts on might be given larger sets or asked to solve problems that involve removing items (counting down).

Another example of a learning trajectory is that children are often able to identify basic shapes before they can articulate the shapes' defining qualities. Once children have a general idea of, and names for, basic shapes, teachers can use activities such as the rope game and the shape hunt, mentioned earlier, to help the children understand the defining characteristics of particular shapes. Children with these understandings might be ready for more complex shapes. Because identifying the next step requires knowing where a child is in relation to typical learning trajectories, activities that provide information about the child's current knowledge and skills are valuable. While math learning trajectories of individual children do not conform exactly to what researchers have summarized as "typical," based on studying large numbers of children, research on trajectories provides some guidance on the order in which new math concepts should be introduced.

Using a curriculum with a research-based scope and sequence can assist teachers in introducing math concepts in an appropriate order, but packaged curricula are not necessary (and not all packaged curricula are based on sound research). Many schools and teachers develop their own math activities based on standards and research on math learning trajectories. And even if a school uses a packaged curriculum, teachers can supplement it with their own activities, those developed by colleagues, or ones found on the internet. Curricula can serve as helpful resources, but teachers know their own students better than curriculum developers, and they need to make adaptations to meet their students' needs and use materials and strategies that make sense within the children's social and cultural contexts.

Teachers occasionally say that administrators pressure them to follow a strict pacing guide connected to the curriculum they use, moving to new concepts based on the time of year rather than children's mastery. Pacing guides are designed to ensure that all of the material is covered and that teachers give all children access to a rigorous curriculum. But pacing guides do not guarantee that all children achieve the ultimate learning goals. Some children begin far behind their age-mates or are not yet proficient in the language of instruction. Others enter the classroom having already mastered the knowledge and skills they are expected to obtain by the end of the year. Strict adherence to pacing guides often results in instruction that is too hard for some children and too easy for others. Teachers required to use pacing

By understanding how their own students learn best, teachers can plan engaging, playful activities that help move children's thinking forward and respond to their individual strengths and needs.

guides can usually make adaptations within the context of particular math skills, such as by varying the difficulty level of the problems they give children or making manipulatives available to children to solve problems. Providing some extra instruction with small groups of children—for example, those who need more support or additional challenges—is another strategy to help meet students' diverse needs.

Conclusion

Standards and accountability have value, but we must make sure they do not get in the way of child-centered, developmentally appropriate, playful learning. The kind of teaching described in this chapter requires teachers to be intentional, to plan lessons carefully, and to provide direct guidance, at least for some math activities. But as the examples illustrate, children are not likely to notice any difference between playing and learning mathematics concepts and skills.

Try This!

› Plan a playful activity to extend children's understanding about early mathematics concepts (e.g., categorization, counting, cardinality, shape concepts). How will the activity support the learning goal? How will you adjust the demands of the task to be appropriate for different skill levels? How will you determine whether the activity was effective?

› Make materials that lend themselves to math activities (e.g., card and board games, sorting activities) easily available to children. Observe what they do with them and try out strategies for encouraging engagement with the materials that will support math learning.

› Give children a math activity to do in pairs (e.g., sorting materials, playing a card game, finding all the rectangles in the classroom). Observe children's social behaviors (e.g., negotiating the task, taking turns, winning or losing gracefully) and consider ways you can promote their social skills in the context of other math activities.

› Observe children during free play and find ways to encourage math learning, such as asking them how many times they can bounce the ball when they are outside, which train is the longest, or how many more blocks one tower has than another one.

naeyc®
Accreditation
Early Learning Programs

This chapter supports the following NAEYC Early Learning Program Accreditation Standards and topic areas:

Standard 1: Relationships
1.F Promoting Self-Regulation

Standard 2: Curriculum
2.A Essential Characteristics
2.B Social and Emotional Development
2.F Early Mathematics

Standard 3: Teaching
3.G Using Instruction to Deepen Children's Understanding and Build Their Skills and Knowledge

Young African American boys are often left behind in mathematics, an essential content area for future school success and careers. Fostering positive math outcomes for them, and for every child, requires self-reflection on your part. Do you hold high expectations for *all* the children you work with? How well do you understand the children's cultural contexts? What mathematical concepts and skills might individual children be ready to learn next? The goal is to make math activities, including those that invite independent exploration in the math center, a magnet for learners so that math is approachable and enjoyable yet sufficiently challenging. Keeping the idea of playful learning in mind, what materials and activities will be appealing to the children you work with and engage them in higher-order thinking and problem-solving experiences—and set them on a positive course for the future?

6

Fostering Positive Experiences in the Math Center for African American Boys

Danielle B. Davis and Dale C. Farran

In a prekindergarten classroom in an impoverished section of the city, Ms. Shepherd announced to the children that they were all going for a walk in the neighborhood. The classroom theme for that month was buildings.

During the walk, the class came upon a house under renovation where the construction workers and electricians were happy to take a break to talk to the children. The children paid rapt attention to measurement, construction plans, and plumb lines and levels. Over the next few weeks, Ms. Shepherd and the children returned to the building site several times, observing from a safe vantage point as the house took shape, cheering on the carpenters.

Back in the classroom, interest in construction was high, and the children engaged in a variety of hands-on activities centered on buildings. With Ms. Shepherd modeling the building process, the class constructed plans to build and design a birdhouse. Each week Ms. Shepherd introduced new ideas around buildings, connecting them to the questions and observations that arose from the class's visit to the construction site.

The teacher also provided mathematical tools in the math center for the children to use as they planned, measured, and constructed. Several children created buildings in the block area, taking tools and measuring devices from the math center to help with their construction. Ms. Williams, the teacher assistant, outlined a skyline of the city for the dramatic play area, and the children added windows and other touches to the mural. The class also interviewed a father who worked for a construction company, and he spent one morning showing the children the basics of how to measure and assemble a house. Throughout the class's building theme, mathematical content was integrated everywhere!

While young children often eagerly play in the dramatic play, art, and block areas, they may have little interest in exploring the math center without prompting. As university-based researchers and consultants, we spent a year intensively observing the math centers in eight publicly funded prekindergarten classrooms in a southern US city. We sought to understand children's natural interactions with math manipulatives and materials during center time. All of the classrooms were relatively well supplied with math-related materials, but in some cases the centers were not set up to foster children's sustained interest or develop their mathematics understanding. Materials were similar across classrooms, but they did not change over time and were not organized in ways that provoked students' curiosity or attention.

Two major research findings support the importance of mathematics learning in urban prekindergarten classrooms that primarily serve children of color. One is that early math

knowledge is a strong predictor of later school success—in reading as well as math (Duncan et al. 2007). The other is that racial disparities in children's math achievement are present at kindergarten entry (Friedman-Krauss 2016)—and these gaps remain large throughout elementary, middle, and high school (National Assessment of Educational Progress [NAEP] 2015).

In this chapter, we argue that creating engaging early math-learning opportunities is critical, especially for African American boys, and we recommend ways teachers can choose materials and design environments to optimize early math learning.

Supporting African American Boys

At an early age, African American boys become aware of racialized stereotypes regarding their own math abilities (Nasir & Shah 2011). On average, African American boys are overrepresented in negative educational outcomes and underrepresented in positive outcomes. Although it is well established that these disparities are due to a wide range of issues regarding opportunities to learn (see Bowman, Comer, & Johns 2018), a misperception remains among some members of the public (including some educators) that these disparities are due to innate differences in abilities. As a result, many African American boys are often confronted with lowered expectations *even when they are high achieving* (Berry III 2008; Zilanawala et al. 2017). Lowered expectations can lead to these children being denied access to rigorous math curricula, feeling unsupported in their math trajectories, and developing a negative attitude toward (or perception of) their abilities to do math—that is, their self-efficacy (Berry III 2008; Nasir & Shah 2011). Making matters worse, new research finds that young children's attitudes toward math are a powerful predictor of their achievement, even after controlling for cognitive abilities (Chen et al. 2018; Digitale-Stanford 2018).

Early exposure to high-quality math environments is increasingly important in determining students' career trajectories.

Setting expectations and attitudes aside, research also finds clear disparities in access to high-quality math learning across educational settings. Young children of color attending urban schools in low-income areas tend to have fewer opportunities to master math knowledge. A study of urban prekindergarten classes showed that math teaching and activities take place much less frequently than literacy teaching and activities (Farran et al. 2017). Studies have also found that in the elementary grades (and beyond), African Americans are underrepresented in gifted programs. For example, a careful examination of gifted referrals in kindergarten, first grade, and third grade found that when Black children had a Black teacher, they were far more likely to be referred and assigned to gifted programs than when they had a non-Black teacher (Grissom & Redding 2016). Given these disparities in opportunities to learn throughout early childhood and elementary school, perhaps it should come as no surprise that, according to the National Assessment of Educational Progress (2015), only 13 percent of African American eighth-grade boys were proficient in math, compared with 43 percent proficiency among White boys.

Early exposure to high-quality math environments is increasingly important in determining students' career trajectories. In 2002, according to the National Science Foundation (NSF), African American college students received only 7 percent of the science, technology, engineering, and mathematics (STEM) bachelor's degrees awarded. In 2014, this percentage remained roughly unchanged. While STEM careers have typically been male dominated, this is not the case among African Americans. Fewer than half of the STEM degrees awarded to African Americans in 2014 went to males (NSF 2017).

African American males' accomplishments in mathematics remain an underresearched topic, especially from an early childhood perspective. Many successful African American men who have STEM careers have attributed their achievement largely to positive early math experiences. This suggests that by offering more challenging and supportive math learning environments, especially when children are young, teachers can improve children's math proficiency and, over time, open doors to STEM careers (Berry III 2008; McGee & Pearman II 2014; Zilanawala et al. 2017).

Providing engaging early math experiences is not simple, however. Significant efforts—such as reducing teacher turnover, increasing spending, and hiring more qualified teachers—have had little impact on improving African American males' math trajectories (Zilanawala et al. 2017). Increasing math involvement in early childhood classrooms serving children of color from low-income families requires fundamentally rethinking math learning opportunities.

Choosing Appropriate Math Materials

Based on questions from teachers, and on the day-to-day challenges we observed in their classrooms, we developed the following guidelines and strategies for selecting appropriate math materials and using them in enriching ways. Teachers should be mindful of children's unique interests and abilities as they structure the math learning environment.

Provide Sequential Activities

In early childhood, the most effective math materials involve sequential learning. Sequential materials give children a logical order or sequence of steps to follow and often involve children creating a working plan, or blueprint, of how they will accomplish the task. Using these types of materials, children engage in higher-order thinking, planning, reflecting, and problem solving. More engagement in sequential activities is linked to higher gains during preschool in both math and self-regulation skills (Farran et al. 2017). Teachers can spark children's interest in sequential materials by introducing and modeling the materials before setting them out for children to independently engage with. For 3- to 5-year-olds, provide materials like tangrams (matching patterns of increasing complexity), peg-sorting boards, and learning cubes with design cards (3-D construction based on 2-D pictures).

Select Materials that Give Children Feedback

While teacher-directed math instruction is important, math centers offer great opportunities for children to explore and learn independently. One way to do this is to provide materials that automatically provide feedback (sometimes called autodidactic or self-correcting), allowing children to independently see when they have gone off course and need to rethink their approach. A simple example is a jigsaw puzzle with pieces that fit together only one way. The self-correcting feature allows children to consistently reinforce their initial ideas about math, leading to sustained math learning and enhanced working memory (Kirschner, Sweller, & Clark 2006; Willingham 2017). Activities like these also may challenge children to try more and more difficult materials as they succeed. One way to maintain children's interest in sequential materials is to scaffold the complexity of the material over time. For example, initially you might have children use the numerals 1–10 in a number game, then expand to 1–20 once they have grasped the concept.

When choosing math materials, consider how much support children are likely to need in order to understand and learn from the activity. It is reasonable to introduce a material and provide occasional support, but if children are likely to need continual guidance, the material may be more appropriate for a small group or one-on-one activity.

Offer Problem-Solving Opportunities

Extending children's initial interest in mathematical activities involves setting high expectations and inviting children to make sense of the world through problem solving. Positive early math experiences are a wonderful way to foster young children's natural curiosity. In our observations, we have found that boys are often attracted to open-ended building materials such as LEGO bricks, Bamboo Building Blocks, and Magna-Tiles because they allow for exploration and creativity. However, children often need some adult assistance to use these materials in ways that provoke more complex thinking. Teachers should scaffold children's play by asking thoughtful questions, increasing challenges, and sparking new explorations over time. They can also encourage children to share their discoveries and their thinking with each other.

Materials such as LEGO bricks and Magna-Tiles allow students to plan elaborate structures with some teacher assistance. For example, a teacher might help a child draw his plans and choose appropriate materials, then later ask detailed, open-ended questions about the child's structure. Pictured (on page 75) is a young boy independently engaged in building stairs for a structure. To determine the height of the stairs, he measured the stairs against the height of the LEGO container. This required the boy to complete several

Why Is Math So Important?

Exposure to high-quality early math experiences and environments allows children to plan, focus, and build on past experiences—actions that develop *executive function skills*. These skills include the ability to suppress distracting information, shift attention between multiple components of a task, and retain and process information, all of which facilitate learning and performance in the classroom (Clements, Sarama, & Germeroth 2016; Fitzpatrick et al. 2014). Engaging in math activities—like playing board games and sorting toys into sets (by color, shape, etc.)—enriches these essential skills.

The connection between math and executive function is especially important for children growing up in homes with low income and underresourced communities, which as of 2016 included 34 percent of Black children (Annie E. Casey Foundation 2018). Recent neurological evidence shows that the areas of the brain most affected by early exposure to poverty are the ones related to executive function skills and reasoning (Noble et al. 2015). Because children from low-income families and underresourced communities tend to have less-predictable routines and be exposed frequently to high-stress environments, they are less likely than children from wealthier families to have well-developed executive function and math skills (Ursache & Noble 2016). Boys in particular have a hard time focusing and persisting without strong environmental support, and boys from low-income, high-stress households have the most difficulty. Younger children are more dependent on the organization of the environment than older children.

It is important to note that environmental support does *not* mean more teacher direction and control. Often, it means creating a math learning center that has enticing materials that support early math skills, minimal distractions, and accessible organization to facilitate children's attention. It can also mean that teachers support and extend children's mathematical ideas by providing comments, questions, and suggestions as children explore the materials. The choice of materials matters (as outlined in the chapter), with some offering more support for learning than others.

Extending children's initial interest in mathematical activities involves setting high expectations and inviting children to make sense of the world through problem solving.

| Step 1: Creating stairs for his structure | Step 2: Measuring the stairs against the tub | Step 3: Transferring the stairs to the structure |

phases of rebuilding and remeasuring to ensure that the stairs fit the structure properly. After several attempts, he was able to transfer the stairs to the structure, and the stairs fit. Play like this—involving complex problem solving—is essential to developing the executive function skills (e.g., shifting attention between multiple components of a task) discussed in "Why Is Math So Important?" (page 73). While solving this challenge, the child remained deeply engaged in his project for the remainder of math center time (roughly half an hour). Providing models (like a laminated poster of stairs) with corresponding plans to follow and suggestions from the teacher can help children enjoy the cognitive benefits—and fun—of more sophisticated play.

Add a Variety of Explicit Math Content

In the prekindergarten classrooms we observed, many of the materials in math centers were variations of sorting and block building. But there is much more to math learning than these two activities. Moreover, sorting and building can happen without children actually learning much math. Boys may be attracted to these types of activities, but the math center should represent a wide range of math content, from patterns to counting and cardinality to spatial relations. Materials that do not at first seem math related can become so with the addition of supporting resources. For example, we have observed that children often use counting bears for dramatic play. If children do not know how to count, having counting bears will not, by itself, teach them. However, providing a lazy Susan with numerals or dots (or a combination of either with color coding) with the counting bears can provide children with actual math learning. The lazy Susan allows children to physically count the quantity of counting bears and match it to the quantity of dots displayed on the lazy Susan (i.e., one-to-one correspondence).

Incorporating STEM into Early Learning

Realizing that all young children have enormous capacity for STEM learning can go a long way toward intentionally providing opportunities for that learning. You can incorporate engaging STEM practices in your classroom in simple ways—you don't have to be an expert, and STEM can happen as part of children's play and other activities you are already doing.

You Don't Have to Be an Expert

Many people believe that supporting STEM learning means having STEM expertise. But, as in other academic domains, learning happens best for young children in the context of play. Educators do not need to be STEM experts but instead can support children's growth by encouraging and practicing STEM habits of mind, like curiosity, exploration, and natural experimentation. By combining hands-on explorations with stories and questions that inspire curiosity, you provide children with opportunities to develop conceptual understanding, acquire new facts, and engage in essential skills such as observing, forming hypotheses, collecting evidence, revising hypotheses, and devising experiments (NSTA 2014). Children develop STEM understandings and habits of mind as they act on their curiosity while playing and interacting with their everyday environments, supported by adults.

An effective STEM teacher often resists directly answering children's questions. Ask purposeful questions and then support children as they investigate for themselves. This fosters self-reliance and resilience, two characteristics that are foundational to STEM inquiry and practices (Van Meeteren & Zan 2010).

Supporting children's curiosity and self-direction requires intention and practice. Learn to facilitate children's open and focused exploration, and encourage them to reflect on their experiences through representation and talking over their ideas (Hoisington 2010). One of your most important roles in encouraging children's natural STEM capacities is to help children persist when they might otherwise give up. When a child encounters frustration, avoid the temptation to resolve the tension with an answer. Instead, help the child develop persistence by showing enthusiasm about the challenge, modeling wonder and curiosity. Ask questions that reengage her intrinsic desire to understand the issue. In contrast to questions that imply a single correct answer (e.g., "Did the ball go up or down?"), questions that encourage experimentation (such as "What do you think would happen if . . .?") help children persist, problem solve, and experience the wonder of discovery (Hoisington 2010). When you get into the habit of asking questions like these, you may find that you yourself enjoy this experience of encouraging children to dig deeper.

STEM Can Happen Within Your Existing Curriculum

The concepts, vocabulary, and habits of mind children develop when they engage in STEM activities are transferable. The activities therefore strengthen many skills, including literacy and attention development. In other words, STEM learning is not an additional task to include on top of other demands: When you view early STEM learning as the development of both knowledge and inquiry-based habits of mind, you discover ways to infuse STEM practices and concepts into your existing curriculum.

For example, STEM and literacy skills go hand in hand. Many of the books you already read aloud to children include STEM-like features: a problem to be solved, an evidence-driven solution that is attempted (and often iterated and reattempted), and the discovery of a method that works. Use these opportunities to illustrate that STEM is everywhere and that there is inherent drama to STEM exploration.

Explicit STEM-based activities can be used to enhance children's engagement and understanding of narratives as well. For example, one preschool class was exploring the book *Lost and Found,* by Oliver Jeffers, about a lost penguin finding his way home on a boat. Teachers asked the 3-year-olds to build and test boats made from aluminum foil to transport a small penguin figure across the water table. The children were deeply engaged in this immersive and meaningful STEM experience, which enhanced their experience with the book and encouraged them to talk at length about the story (Draper & Wood 2017).

Once you start to embed these approaches to supporting children's explorations, you'll be in a prime position to help families and other educators see the remarkably sophisticated, and often hidden, STEM capacity of young children and to see how powerful early STEM experiences can be in shaping the minds of the next generation.

Adapted from E. McClure, "More Than a Foundation: Young Children Are Capable STEM Learners," 2017, *Young Children* 72 (5): 83–89.

We often saw Bristle Blocks in math centers even though they teach little to no math. While some spatial learning may occur with materials like Bristle Blocks, too often children merely attach them without reference to constructing a shape. For Bristle Blocks to enhance math, teachers need to add some creative suggestions for how children can interact with the blocks. Take advantage of how attractive the blocks are to children by adding measuring tapes, rulers, and suggestions for their usage, giving children a means to use these materials mathematically.

Avoid Materials that Distract from Math Learning

Be aware of the nonmathematical aspects of materials and activities that may compete for children's attention. For example, young children are often distracted by the features of a math manipulative, particularly color, and may have trouble recognizing the mathematical concept (Willingham 2017). Consider if color is being used for mathematical purposes (such as comparing the quantities of red cars and blue cars) or if it is simply a distraction (such as a rainbow of hues in a game intended to focus on one-to-one correspondence or counting on).

It is important to note that materials in which a nonmathematical concept is redundant with the mathematical concept may impair children's math learning. For instance, many materials that aim to focus on sorting allow for both numerical and color sorting; it is very possible for children to sort entirely by color and be correct without attending to the math features at all. In addition, recent research has shown that preschoolers can become

overstimulated by materials with multiple features and can have trouble distinguishing which one is most relevant (Willingham 2017). When materials have multiple features, children may need adult support to identify and attend to the mathematical aspects. For independent learning in math centers, materials with a minimal number of distracting features may be more effective.

Organizing the Environment to Maximize Learning

Young children are highly dependent on the organization of the environment to be able to engage with math materials in a meaningful way. A space that is neatly organized, labeled, and engaging will garner far more attention than a poorly arranged center. When children can easily see all available materials, they can better plan their math-related play, be it building a pyramid or copying a design or sorting toy animals into different types of sets (perhaps by tail length). Maintaining their interest throughout the year requires adding new materials and/or enhancing old materials with new resources that allow children to do more with what is at hand. For example, you could provide children with sets of pattern blocks and simple designs to copy. As the children gain mastery, you can add more complex designs and invite children to create their own using the shapes. Teachers can also expand this design copying using other materials, such as beads or LEGO bricks.

Containers for materials are often labeled to make cleanup easier, but there is a more important benefit to labeling. Appropriately labeling materials with photos and/or text helps children access them easily. Labels can also be enhanced to remind children of more challenging ways to play with the materials. Children can then independently navigate centers, making informed decisions and plans about what supplies to work with. Many materials fit well into tubs that are easy to label. Oddly shaped and large materials can be placed on labeled shelves.

To reengage children and maintain their attention, refresh materials after every unit of study by adding new items and changing the supporting materials. For example, if counters in the math center are used only to practice one-to-one correspondence, you can add pattern cards that prompt children to use the counters in new ways. There is not one prescribed time frame for rotating materials. When you observe fewer children choosing the math center, it's a strong indication that the materials need updating.

Conclusion

Fostering high-quality early math experiences can have a tremendous effect on the long-term school success and career trajectories of African American males. While the guidelines we have outlined here are beneficial to all preschoolers, they are critically important to male children of color. Far too many schools are not providing the vigorous math activities, materials, and supports that children of color need, hampering their opportunities to later engage in advanced math courses or enter STEM-related fields.

Early childhood teachers can foster productive math experiences for African American boys by having positive individual interactions, providing opportunities for exploration, extending children's initial interests, and structuring the environment to continuously attract and engage children in math learning.

The way in which teachers and parents approach and communicate the importance of math learning has a direct link to a young boy's perception of his ability to enjoy and excel in math. It also impacts his self-regulation skills. Therefore, making math a meaningful and inviting experience is vital in all early childhood classrooms—especially those serving African American boys growing up in underresourced communities.

Try This!

> Make a list of resources suggested in the chapter that promote engagement with mathematical concepts (e.g., tangrams, peg sorts, number cubes, design cards, jigsaw puzzles, puzzle boards, color tiles, counting cars and bears, materials for design copying and building, and board and card games). Choose three and jot down what children can learn as they manipulate the materials and play. How might you support and extend their learning?

> Refresh your mathematics materials. Organize your setting with ample table space. Redesign the storage area for easy access with containers that are labeled and have photos of contents. What activities, games, and resources can you add? Think about whether children would benefit more from an introduction to new additions or from simply exploring materials on their own at first.

> Use math talk to solve simple daily problems throughout the day. For example, "Some plates are missing muffins. How many more do we need?" or "How far do you think you are throwing the ball? I wonder how we could measure the distance."

naeyc® Accreditation

Early Learning Programs

This chapter supports the following NAEYC Early Learning Program Accreditation Standards and topic areas:

Standard 2: Curriculum
2.A Essential Characteristics
2.F Early Mathematics

Standard 3: Teaching
3.A Designing Enriched Learning Environments
3.F Making Learning Meaningful for All Children

Rich, creative learning through play often is sparked when teachers introduce a new material to the environment. The addition of an unusual material to this school's playground inspired children to play in many different ways over the course of the school year. Notice how many transformations their play underwent and the different directions it took. How did the teachers facilitate this? In what other ways might learning have been scaffolded and deepened through teacher guidance? What new materials can you introduce to jump-start rich learning through play? Think about ways you can build on children's interests and enthusiasm to extend their learning into other areas of the curriculum.

7

What Can You Do with Bamboo? Preschoolers Explore a Natural Material

Condie Collins Ward

Our play-based preschool playground is certified as an Outdoor Classroom by Nature Explore (www.natureexplore.org), a national nonprofit organization that seeks to help schools and families make nature an integral, joyful part of children's daily learning. Our staff continually look for ways to enrich the space with a variety of natural materials, because we strongly believe that children benefit from having their creativity and imagination stimulated and using all their senses to explore. In recent years, the natural materials we've added to our playground include hay bales, wood cookies, logs, recycled Christmas trees, pinecones, driftwood, rocks, and vines. And one year, bamboo.

Near the beginning of the school year, a staff member heard about free bamboo available from a neighbor and raised the idea of bringing some to the school. Teachers embraced the opportunity to provide the children new experiences with this unique natural material. Within a few days, thirty 6- to 12-foot bamboo poles were brought to the school playground, and we piled them inside the playground in a spot where they wouldn't interfere with the play equipment or surrounding foot traffic areas. Eager to see how the children would react to the new material, and in keeping with the staff's desire for children to create understanding through the process of discovery, the teachers decided to not structure how the bamboo might be used. They would observe the play and language that emerged around the bamboo and support and extend the children's ideas with questions, suggestions, and later on, new materials that might spark further creativity and learning.

What can preschoolers do with bamboo? As it turns out, a lot!

Excitement! Discovering Bamboo

The children first saw the bamboo when they went outdoors for playground time. It was highly visible and striking because of its color and quantity. The pieces were green; some were thick and others were thin, and some shorter ones had leaves still attached. The first explorers were drawn to the pieces with leaves. The children stood these upright, commenting that the stalks were taller than their bodies. They hoisted them up above their heads, touching the highest play equipment, and shouted to one another, "Look! I can reach all the way to the top of the high climber!"

As more and more children got involved in playing with the bamboo, teachers noticed there wasn't enough room for everyone to experiment freely while staying safe. The teachers led some children out to a larger lawn area, where they reached their pieces up to touch tall branches, commenting, "We can reach as high as the trees!" The sticks of bamboo were like arm extensions and gave the children a sense of being tall and mighty. When they shook the leaf-covered stalks, the leaves made a rustling sound. Teachers drew children's attention to the sound: "I hear something when you move the branches. Do you hear it?" The children shook their branches, creating sounds intentionally. They went on to touch all the high places they could find—other tall trees, each other's branches, and a second-story balcony on the school building.

The bigger, leafless pieces of bamboo inspired the children to work together to lift and carry the poles. "Teamwork!" they chanted. Some of the children hopped over poles on the ground, while others tested their jumping skills by raising a pole a few inches off the ground and then jumping over it. A few days after the bamboo arrived, the playground looked like a game of pick-up sticks for giants! When some of the youngest children came to the playground and saw the jumbled pieces of bamboo, they experimented with jumping in and out of the spaces, seeing which ones would fit their bodies. On occasion, teachers noticed bamboo pieces were in the way of children navigating the playground. Together with the children, they moved the pieces to safer places. Teachers brought children's attention to the fact that some pieces could be lifted easily by one person, while other pieces required two or more children to move from one place to another. They encouraged children to ask their friends to help. Throughout the year, the excitement of lifting something big and toting it around never wore off.

As children explored the bamboo, teachers documented children's conversations and actions, noting the challenges that arose and how children arrived at solutions. They also took photos. Teachers reflected on what they saw and heard, and they discussed ways to keep the children safe, how to handle weaponry play with the bamboo, and what additional props they could add to expand the play, such as tires, tree stumps, hay, hollow blocks, and large plastic tubes.

While children played, teachers stayed nearby in case help was needed, paying close attention to make sure everyone was safe. If a child wanted to carry a long pole around the playground, adults intervened so others didn't get bumped in the process. On their own,

What Can You Do with Bamboo? Preschoolers Explore a Natural Material

As children explored the bamboo, teachers documented children's conversations and actions, noting the challenges that arose and how children arrived at solutions.

children did not necessarily understand the potential hazards, so the teachers asked them to think about ways they could keep each other safe when carrying a piece of bamboo. Together, it was agreed that having more children hold the pieces being moved would help. Teachers also suggested that children look in front of and behind themselves to see who might be in the path. Children who wanted to carry a long pole by themselves were encouraged to drag it, while maintaining their awareness of who was nearby. Learning how to transport the material safely was ongoing work. The extended time the bamboo was on our playground enabled children to learn how to move their bodies through space while transporting large objects, be considerate of others, and ask for help when needed.

Creating and Imagining

The children found many ways to use the bamboo. Some of the very youngest children noticed parallel pieces on the ground left behind by another class. Indoors, these same children had been making tracks for their trains and cars. The parallel bamboo poles reminded them of tracks, and some walked and pushed wheelbarrows within the poles as they called out, "Choo-choo!" When teachers asked whether the children wanted to add more tracks to make it bigger, the children rounded up more pieces and extended the tracks by laying pieces end to end. This group effort showed that they shared a common idea of what train tracks look like and how they are used. Teachers supported this play by observing and making verbal observations: "I see Noah's train moving down the tracks! I hear his horn tooting! Does anybody else want to get on the train with Noah?" Others nearby moved inside the tracks to follow Noah. By guiding the children's play and making suggestions within the current story line, the teachers encouraged several children to become involved with this activity. Other groups used the train tracks as roads, and some walked on stilts inside the bamboo lines.

Some children took the bamboo stalks with leaves to the sandbox and attempted to plant one in the sand. They worked collaboratively to dig a hole in the ground. The stalk fell over in their early attempts. Teachers encouraged the children to rethink their plan by describing what they saw and asking questions: "Hmm, you dug a hole together and planted the branch in it, but the branch keeps falling over. Does anyone have an idea of how we could make the branch stand up in the sand so that it won't fall over?" After some experimentation and sharing of ideas, the children discovered that they had to plant it deeper to secure it. "You have to dig a deep hole!" they said to each another.

Noticing how invested children were in digging a single hole, teachers encouraged them to dig other holes for more branches. The children had previously planted plastic flowers in the sand and helped plant real vegetables in planters at the school. Some had also done gardening with their families. The bamboo branches were many times bigger than what they had worked with in those experiences. By investigating the properties of the environment and adapting their play to solve problems, the children were able to carry out their ideas

successfully. They spoke of their finished work as a "beautiful forest." The teachers built on Dewey's belief that "a child's own instincts and powers furnish the material and give the starting point for all education" (1897, 77).

One day, a child spontaneously decided to lean one of the long pieces of bamboo against a tree on the playground. Others joined him, forming a tepee-like structure around the tree's base. This group effort continued until they had used all the available bamboo poles. Once the structure was completed, the children went in and out of it, with some referring to it as their "clubhouse." Noticing that the ground inside the structure was damp, teachers encouraged the children to gather pine needles to make a dry floor. Everyone got involved in loading up wagons and transporting needles to the structure. The children also added log sections, which they rolled into the space for seats. Some chose to make a campfire out of sticks. The final structure was big enough for multiple children to play inside. The bamboo tepee mirrored previous stick structures the children had created.

The presence of the bamboo opened up some potentially risky situations, and the teachers had to decide how much risk was desirable in order to let the children stretch their abilities and expand their play, and how risk could be mitigated. The teachers tied some of the longest poles to play structures to add visual interest and height, and one of these poles was fastened adjacent to a tall slide. A child started to climb up the pole, and a teacher quickly stepped in to help that child shinny up the pole and shift from there onto the lower part of the slide to slide safely down. Seeing this, others wanted to try it too. But teachers were concerned that without an adult's help, the pole might slip or not hold a child's weight. Instead of taking the pole down or telling the children it was off-limits for climbing, the teachers collaborated with the children to find a way to make the activity as safe as possible for all who wanted to try it. Teachers listened to the children's ideas ("We'll only go partway up" and "We can slide down the slide to get off") and decided that this risk was advantageous. As Gray relates, "Children climb trees and other structures to scary heights, from which they gain a birds-eye view of the world and the thrilling feeling of 'I did it!'" (2014). To keep children as safe as possible, however, teachers explained that this activity could take place only with the assistance of an adult.

The teachers had to decide how much risk was desirable in order to let the children stretch their abilities and expand their play.

Expanding the Play and Prompting Thinking

Throughout the year, teachers looked for possibilities to extend the children's play and learning. They introduced other materials for children to use with the bamboo, including pieces of gauzy fabric, hay bales, and recycled Christmas trees. The gauzy fabric was tied to the tepee to make it look different. Looking through the gauzy fabric, children inside the structure pretended they were ghosts by leaning against the fabric and making ghostlike sounds. Children played with the hay bales and later, when the hay bales started to come apart, added that hay to the floor of the tepee. Multiple recycled Christmas trees that were scattered across the playground provided opportunities for the children to poke bamboo poles through the middle of the trees, watching as they came out the other side.

Teachers also deliberately prompted play by fashioning equipment with the bamboo. Encasing a strong bamboo pole in a heavy-duty plastic tube, they invited children to sit on the pole and bounce gently, with one teacher on either end.

Teachers observed the children using the bamboo and solving problems in a number of other ways:

> Pretending to saw stalks with play chainsaws, including making sounds of saws cutting

> Fashioning spyglasses from two short pieces held side by side

> Tapping on logs with shorter pieces (Noticing the sound the bamboo made when it struck the log, children called out, "I made a drum!")

Teachers also offered comments and posed questions to find out what the children were thinking and to prompt ideas.

> Writing in the dirt: "Tyler, I see you wrote your name! How did you make the letters?"

> Putting long pieces on top of the playhouse roof: "Wow! How did those get up there?" (This was followed by children demonstrating their abilities and saying, "Like this!")

> Rescuing stuck Frisbees from tall trees: "How will we reach that high? Can you think of something long that we can use?"

> Reaching through the fence to poke ice-crusted puddles: "What do you notice?"

As fall turned into winter, the bamboo started to look different, changing from green to light tan. Adults and children gradually became aware of this change. Teachers saw an opportunity to prompt children's thinking about the effects of natural processes and the changes that take place in nature over time. They asked the children to think about what the bamboo had looked like when it first came to the playground, and whether they noticed anything different about it now.

The children offered their assessments: "It was green before" and "Now it looks light brown." Pondering this, they asked the teachers why it had changed color. Teachers encouraged them to think about possible reasons. The children were unsure. Teachers noted that the bamboo was always outside, exposed to sun and heat, cold, rain, and snow. "Do you think that might have something to do with it changing color?" they asked. While children didn't know for sure, their expressions indicated they were turning over the idea in their heads. Teachers made a point of not giving an instant right answer to children's inquiries. They believed that given some time and additional prompting, the children might come to their own conclusions and understandings.

Sharing the Play and Learning with Families

A month or so into the children's bamboo exploration, some families had questions and concerns about the bamboo. They wondered how the children were using the material and whether the play was safe. We realized that parents needed information and support to understand why we felt that playing with the bamboo was important for the children.

We shared documentation that showed all the ways the children used the bamboo (see "What Did Children Learn from Bamboo Play?"), and we listed the many areas of development and learning that were impacted:

> Small and large motor skills

> Creativity and inventiveness

> Collaboration

> Social interactions and role-playing

> Math and scientific knowledge

> Vocabulary and more

What Did Children Learn from Bamboo Play?

We use the Connecticut Preschool Assessment Framework as one way to assess children's learning (Connecticut State Department of Education 2008). The children's explorations with bamboo connected to the following performance standards.

Personal and Social

The children

> Showed self-direction with a range of materials

> Sustained attention to task/goal (constructing a tepee)

> Followed rules set out for safety ("Watch as you carry long poles so you don't bump anyone")

> Interacted cooperatively with peers (reaching a Frisbee stuck in a tree)

Physical

The children

> Used large motor movements (shinnying up a pole, lifting pieces)

Cognitive

The children

> Engaged in scientific inquiry (leaning bamboo poles in different ways against a tree to create a stable structure)

> Engaged in observation (noticing the bamboo's change of color over time)

> Used a variety of strategies to solve problems (calling to friends for help with the long poles—"Teamwork!")

> Compared/ordered objects ("That pole is longer than this pole," "Those have leaves and these don't")

> Demonstrated spatial awareness (reaching high with long poles, going under the pole)

> Used complex sentences/vocabulary to describe ideas/experiences (discussing bamboo play at the morning meetings)

> Engaged in conversations about bamboo

> Wrote their names in the dirt with bamboo sticks

Creative Expression

The children

> Constructed structures to fit with their play and represent their own ideas (laying train tracks, poking poles through Christmas trees)

> Represented experiences/fantasies in play (creating a "campfire" in the tepee, using bamboo train tracks and roads)

> Discovered musical properties of bamboo as they tapped it with sticks

The bamboo remained available for children to play with every day after school, and parents and children often stayed to play on the playground. Responding to parents' concerns about how to assist their children in using the bamboo in safe ways, we installed holders for the bamboo on the fencing, and at the end of each day, teachers and children put it away. We had conversations with parents about how they—like teachers—needed to watch their children carefully while they used the bamboo after school. We offered parents the option of telling their children the bamboo was closed after school if they didn't want their children to play with it. We relayed any information about the bamboo in conversations with families on the playground at drop-off and pickup times, as well as in weekly newsletters, where we also detailed the children's experiences with the bamboo.

Inspiring New Possibilities

About midway through the year the children had become really familiar with the long bamboo pieces, and we noticed that interest in playing with them had waned. Considering how we might revitalize interest, we asked the head of maintenance at the school to cut some of the bamboo poles into different lengths. Using a table saw, he had children help by holding the poles steady while he made cuts. The children took turns being helpers. Some waited in nearby chairs and watched until it was their turn. Others were uncomfortable being near the loud sound of the saw yet wanted to see what was happening, so they sat a little farther away. Seeing a familiar adult using a power tool that transformed the bamboo into something different was of great interest, prompting comments about what was happening and what they might do with the new, shorter pieces.

Finding the edges of the cut bamboo somewhat sharp, the teachers decided to sand them. They enlisted the children's help and illustrated how to smooth the rough spots using small pieces of sandpaper. This was intriguing and prompted comparisons of rough and smooth surfaces and ideas about how rubbing the surface of the bamboo changed its texture.

Once in a while, children wielded the poles like weapons. Wanting to encourage children to play in a variety of ways, the teachers brainstormed ideas about how to address this use of the bamboo poles. Engaging with and encouraging a child to find another way to play with the bamboo was sometimes successful; teachers made suggestions if a child needed help coming up with a different idea. Steering a child to find a friend to collaborate with and create something completely different sometimes shifted the play from using weapons to building. Sometimes a teacher worked with a child to come up with a safe way the child could fulfill his desire to use the bamboo as a weapon that would not hurt or frighten other children. With a child who was swinging the pole, the teacher offered, "You can swing the pole if we go to a more open area where there are no people who could get bumped." Teachers experimented with different strategies depending on the children and situations involved. There were also occasions when we had to tell children they could not

Transforming
the bamboo
into something
different
prompted
comments
from children
about what
was happening
and what
they might do
with the new,
shorter pieces.

use bamboo for the rest of the day. When that happened, we had them help us put it away and then join other activities. Consistently implementing these approaches avoided much of the bamboo weaponry play.

The teachers took time at daily class meetings to discuss the children's bamboo play. They elicited children's feedback on what had happened on a given day. Together, children and teachers celebrated discoveries (Children: "We made a clubhouse!") and brainstormed challenges (Teachers: "We noticed that poles on the ground are tripping people. What can we do to solve this problem?"). By getting children's input and implementing their ideas, teachers helped them have ownership of the material.

The bamboo stayed on our playground all year and provided months of exploration for the preschool children. The long exposure gave children a chance to revisit, rework, rethink, troubleshoot, construct, and discover. As the pieces started to break down over time due to sun, heat, cold, and moisture, teachers took the splintery-looking pieces that were no longer safe to play with and turned them into flagpoles that they tied to the fence. On windy days, colorful cloth triangle flags waved in the breeze—yet another imaginative use of bamboo!

Try This!

> Prepare ample open-ended materials for children to explore and use in their play (e.g., cartons, empty plastic bottles, cardboard tubes, natural materials, unusual tools and containers, loose parts for tinkering and construction, and interesting collections). Invite families to contribute materials. Notice how children use the materials. What suggestions can you make to prompt additional ideas and help children look at things in a new way?

> Ask children what materials they might need for the activities they're engaging in. As they play, occasionally ask, "What else do you need?" Modify and add materials to extend children's ideas and interest over time.

> Evaluate the level of challenge present in children's current play, and encourage more complex play. For example, add tools, provide a digital camera, and introduce books and photographs to reflect a topic or theme. What questions can you ask to prompt more complex experimentation with building, tinkering, or imaginative play?

> What goals for scientific inquiry, mathematics, language, social and emotional development, creative expression, and physical development will be supported by materials and suggestions you provide?

naeyc Accreditation
Early Learning Programs

This chapter supports the following NAEYC Early Learning Program Accreditation Standards and topic areas:

Standard 2: Curriculum
2.A Essential Characteristics
2.D Language Development
2.F Early Mathematics
2.G Science

Standard 3: Teaching
3.A Designing Enriched Learning Environments
3.E Responding to Children's Interests and Needs

Standard 7: Families
7.B Sharing Information Between Staff and Families

The authors of this chapter share their journey with a small group of teachers as the teachers grow to see the value of providing more time for child-directed approaches to learning. Notice how the teachers asked specific questions to draw children's attention to new ideas. How did they encourage peer collaboration? How did they build on dual language learners' experiences when they introduced and defined new vocabulary? Consider Ms. Hall's decision to support the children's interest rather than continue with her own plan. In such situations, what do you use to help you make a decision? Wherever you are in your own journey of observing, planning, and guiding in order to most effectively help all children learn, document how the children respond to different types of learning situations. How can you use this information to advocate for a more child-centered approach to teaching?

8

Engaging and Enriching Play Is Rigorous Learning

**Shannon Riley-Ayers and
Alexandra Figueras-Daniel**

In a time of accountability, push-down, and high-stakes assessments (even in some kindergarten classrooms!), many early childhood educators feel pressured to focus on academic rigor—often with instructional practices that are not developmentally appropriate. A misconception among some educators, administrators, parents, and policy makers is that a narrow definition of academic rigor—one that emphasizes worksheets and other highly teacher-directed activities—is especially necessary for children growing up in underresourced communities. Research shows that a more beneficial approach is to offer an even richer, more well-rounded education in which children have meaningful, frequent opportunities to be self-directed scholars (Adair 2014; Lerkkanen et al. 2016). With the right supports, young children flourish when provided opportunities to be engaged in investigations that integrate content. In addition, it is important to immerse children in an educational environment that maximizes use of academic English to build knowledge about the world (Snow 2017).

Developing academic vocabulary is critical. In later grades, decoding problems are relatively rare, but comprehension problems—driven by lack of vocabulary and background knowledge—are rampant (Snow & Matthews 2016). Rigor and developmentally appropriate practice are both essential to early childhood education; done well, they are mutually reinforcing (Brown, Feger, & Mowry 2015). This may be a bold claim, but consider the transformation of 17 kindergarten classrooms from didactic experiences for children to rigorous and developmentally appropriate student-centered learning environments. See these changes through the eyes of one partner teacher, and the formal and informal classroom observation data that documented these changes. Throughout this chapter, the focus is on practices that support children's language and knowledge growth, using vignettes and reflections to provide meaningful examples of how to build on children's activities and interests.

Working *with* Teachers

Our goal for kindergarten teachers in one urban district in New Jersey was developmentally appropriate academic rigor for all students. The city that the district serves is 72 percent Hispanic, with 81 percent of families reporting Spanish as their home language. A total of 40 percent of children under age 18 in the city are living in poverty, and 100 percent of students in the school district qualify for free or reduced-price lunch (ACNJ 2016). Census data from 2015 show that less than 33 percent of 18- to 24-year-olds in the city attend college or complete an associate's degree.

The school district currently receives state preschool aid dollars as part of legislation in New Jersey that mandates that all 3- and 4-year-olds living in the state's lowest-income districts have access to full-day, high-quality preschool programs. Although thorough evaluations (Barnett et al. 2013) have demonstrated that these preschool programs are effective, the district's state-mandated standardized reading and math test results remain worrisome. In 2016, just 20 percent of third-graders met expectations in English language arts (ELA) and 25 percent met expectations for math. These results are far below the state third-grade averages for meeting expectations—41 percent in ELA and 39 percent in math (NJ ED 2017). The takeaway is

clear: While attendance in high-quality preschool shows great value, there is a need to focus on teaching and learning quality in subsequent grades to build on gains made in preschool (Stipek et al. 2017).

As active participants in this work, we engaged directly with practitioners throughout the school system to shift the mindset and practices to blend the required academic rigor with a more developmentally appropriate approach. As former early childhood teachers, we were able to draw on our experiences and expertise to guide both administrators and teachers through a transformation that demonstrated research results of increased teaching quality.

To catalyze changes in kindergarten teaching practices, the coaches (the second author and another qualified former practitioner) needed to gain the teachers' trust and secure their commitment; the teachers had to believe that transformation in their classrooms was critical to the students they served—and possible to accomplish. Like many teachers, these teachers were suffering from initiative fatigue (Reeves 2010). Understandably, as initiatives come and go, teachers often become ambivalent about investing effort into each new educational shift.

To combat this fatigue, we aimed to support teachers and empower them to use their professional decision making in the classroom. To accomplish this, both authors partnered with administrative staff (building and central office) to boost administrators' understanding of the best teaching practices and to initiate policy revisions, including providing teachers the professional discretion to change their practices.

The teachers, full of desire to succeed, at first wanted a script or a step-by-step recipe. One teacher explained, "We've piloted programs before where we were told exactly what to do and say. I think that's why our mindset is just 'tell us what to do and how to do it.'" We had no intention of providing a script. The core of our approach is guiding and facilitating change through a process of self-reflection. Our intervention would support the teachers' pedagogical approaches and understanding of teaching and learning.

Research has found that teachers' use of two instructional strategies—using sophisticated vocabulary and giving sustained attention while talking with students during free play—in preschool and kindergarten is related to fourth-grade reading comprehension and decoding skills (Dickinson & Porche 2011). These findings are critically important, as reading is the foundation for most learning in education and in life. Equally important is the educational setting: Neither of these instructional strategies can be practiced if there is not sufficient time to spend with children in student-selected and student-directed centers. Driven by this research, our work with the teachers focused on helping them to broaden children's background knowledge with language and to follow children's leads in creating learning activities that were rigorous and developmentally appropriate.

Broadening Background Knowledge with Language

During center time, Paola (a dual language learner) approaches Ms. Hall, the teacher, with a playdough pie and proudly says, "Look! I made a cake! It's blueberry." Ms. Hall responds, "Oh, I think you made a pie!" Paola exclaims, "Yes!"

This appears to be the end of the exchange, so Ms. Figueras-Daniel, the coach, interjects, "I love this design you put on the top! It reminds me of warm blueberry pie. My mom used to make this for me in the summer, when I was a little girl like you." Paola smiles.

Ms. Figueras-Daniel continues, "Have you ever had a piece of pie?" Paola shakes her head to signal that she has not.

Ms. Figueras-Daniel asks, "Do you know what this design is called on top of your pie?"

Paola answers, with a smile, "Lines."

Ms. Figueras-Daniel responds, "Yes, and those lines make a lattice. See how each line overlaps the other?" Paola nods, and Ms. Figueras-Daniel continues, "This is the crust of the pie. The crust is made of sweet dough that keeps the fruit filling inside. When you bake it, it gets crunchy or crusty."

Paola says, "I make more pie."

Ms. Figueras-Daniel and Ms. Hall follow Paola back to the playdough table and work alongside her, rolling playdough flat and cutting it into strips. Ms. Figueras-Daniel uses Paola's interest to continue teaching vocabulary, building background knowledge, and modeling language: "When you use the dough as a lattice top, like you did, it makes a pretty cover. Sometimes piecrusts cover the whole pie, but then you can't see the filling. That's what's on the inside."

Giving children the freedom to pursue their interests and then building on their ideas is developmentally appropriate for kindergarten and can lead to academically rigorous learning.

The vignette illustrates the importance of extended conversations to build on what children already know, and it shows that meaningful interactions can support students' oral language development. Most significantly, the vignette demonstrates that a teacher must tailor her instruction to address the needs of each child in the classroom. For Paola, a dual language learner, the coach asked more closed-ended questions. This showed that she understood Paola's language abilities in English. She then scaffolded Paola's learning by modeling language and intentionally describing unfamiliar words with concrete, descriptive meanings. As the classroom teacher and coach continued to interact with Paola, other students joined in the discussion about baking.

On a subsequent day, Ms. Hall planned small group time to include reading *The Apple Pie Tree,* by Zoe Hall. She brought in the ingredients and tools necessary to make pie dough and used the recipe at the end of the book to make a pie with the children. The teacher and coach worked with the children to intentionally integrate domains (here, math) by measuring ingredients and naming utensils, such as rolling pins, measuring spoons, and measuring cups. Ms. Hall mapped her actions to words: "See, I am using the smallest measuring spoon to add a tiny bit of baking powder," and "Now I need to roll the dough out to make it flat. I'll need to use the utensil that rolls—the rolling pin." As the group created the latticework on their own in small groups, Ms. Hall talked about other objects that have a lattice design on them, such as fences. The children enjoyed describing the types of fences they see on their walks to school.

Ms. Hall effectively built on students' interest in a topic and further engaged them to introduce novel vocabulary and to learn about the nuanced uses of words such as *lattice.* This type of interaction increases students' background knowledge, an important contributor not only to word learning but also to reading fluency (Priebe, Keenan, & Miller 2011) and reading comprehension in later grades, when texts are more complex (Neuman, Kaefer, & Pinkham 2014). Although pie baking was not represented in the district curriculum, it was evident in these interactions and lessons that learning standards related to oral language development and mathematics (including measurement) were being targeted.

In the Common Core State Standards, and in standards adapted from the Common Core, the increase in practices geared to teaching knowledge rather than teaching individual skills is not accidental (Cervetti & Hiebert 2015). Pairing teacher–child interactions (like Ms. Figueras-Daniel's engagement with Paola around her playdough pie) with reading-related nonfiction and fiction texts (like Ms. Hall's selection of *The Apple Pie Tree*) is necessary for building children's content knowledge—and it is especially important for dual language learners and others who have fewer opportunities to engage with academic English at home. This approach to literacy development allows children to become interested and engaged and to experience vocabulary and concepts from differing perspectives through character voices and varied settings (Camp 2000). Just as important, using student interest to guide interactions and learning allows students to feel valued as members of the classroom community.

Paola's experience exemplifies our premise that giving children the freedom to pursue their interests and then building on their ideas is developmentally appropriate for kindergarten and can lead to academically rigorous learning. Using children's interests and creations to introduce new vocabulary and complex language enables teachers to provide students with a more meaningful and engaging learning experience. In early childhood, complex language skills, such as proper grammar, an extensive definitional vocabulary, and good listening comprehension, have strong relationships with later reading ability, including decoding and reading comprehension (NELP 2008).

While Paola did not yet have the vocabulary in English to elaborate on her pie creation, the adults recognized this and quickly engaged in an interaction that provided a rich array of vocabulary. Doing this is particularly important for dual language learners; structured talk about academically relevant content (rather than rote memorization of word lists) is crucial (Gillanders, Castro, & Franco 2014). Following children's interests in topics provides for rich learning that can build upon their previous knowledge and experiences. Tying in the experience and vocabulary of baking a pie to children's previous experiences and background knowledge made for a stronger connection and deeper learning for Paola and her classmates. If a child has made flan at home or has visited a bakery for bread or a birthday cake, the teacher could use that knowledge to link the new learning. This discussion-based learning around a topic of interest to children allows them to build knowledge and vocabulary across subject areas rather than in isolation. To be highly effective, it is necessary for teachers to model and intentionally teach words' meanings while providing students with multiple opportunities to use the words in context (Takanishi & Le Menestrel 2017). This simply cannot be done in rote exercises such as using flashcards or worksheets.

Developmentally Appropriate Academic Rigor

Ms. Hall plans to study buildings and structures. To gauge students' interests, she begins with an idea web. The students share many ideas, and Juan, a usually reserved dual language learner, suggests igloos. He expresses interest in constructing a model igloo in the classroom, one large enough to use as a hideout for reading books with his classmates. Ms. Hall seems uncertain about this—her aim was for the students to learn about skyscrapers. Their urban school is housed in an old six-story art deco bank building with a rooftop playground that offers interesting views of other buildings in the city and a blurry but definite view of the Manhattan skyline. But the students agree that they want to learn about igloos, so Ms. Hall moves in that direction.

After a few read-alouds on igloos, Ms. Hall uses writer's workshop time for the students to draw and write plans for the igloo they will build. She circulates, commenting on their work and engaging in conversation about the drawings. "What can you tell me about your drawing?" she asks Yousef, who has drawn a spiral-shaped design. Yousef explains that his drawing is what the igloo looks like "on top." Ms. Hall responds, "I see! This is the igloo from above, like how the birds would see it!" Yousef nods excitedly. Ms. Hall says, "We call this a bird's-eye view because of that. When you see things from above, we say it's a bird's-eye view. It definitely looks different from what Juan drew, which is the igloo as we would see it if we were standing in front of it."

The children begin building the igloo with empty gallon jugs. Ms. Hall infuses academic rigor with math and science concepts, such as using a compass to make the initial circle and discussing the number of jugs that might be needed. However, while gluing jugs to form the second and third rows, the children notice that the structure looks like a cylinder—not a dome. In a whole group discussion, Ms. Hall engages the children in solving this problem.

Damian begins almost inaudibly, saying "big to small" while motioning with his hands. Ms. Hall says encouragingly, "Tell us what you mean by 'biggest to smallest.'" Damian motions the dome shape with his hands. "How can we make our igloo get smaller at the top?" asks Ms. Hall, looking at a student holding a small whiteboard. "Maybe if we draw it, we can figure out how to do this." Mateo yells, "It's a circle!" Camila exclaims, "It's a rainbow!" Smiling, Ms. Hall says, "Yes, it's shaped like a rainbow on the outside.

Students had multiple opportunities to think critically by directing their own inquiry, with guidance by the teacher.

Does anyone remember what that shape is called?" After pausing to give the children time to think, she says, "We read a book that had an arc."

Ms. Hall describes the book and the reference to an arc. She uses her hands to show flat versus round to give children a concrete understanding of the new vocabulary. The children exclaim, "It's round!" Ms. Hall says, "Yes! It is round. It is half of a sphere—like if we cut a ball in half. We will have to keep thinking to figure out how to make our igloo take this shape. Do you think we can continue to plan our igloo in the centers?" Damian says that he is going to read a book about it in the library center.

Ms. Hall provided children with opportunities to engage in contextually rich, meaningful conversations that were sustained over several exchanges. Important to note are the multiple opportunities for students to think critically by directing their own inquiry, with guidance by the teacher. The classroom environment played a role as it allowed the students the autonomy to seek materials, tools, paper, pencils, books, and collaboration with peers to carry out their work. The igloo construction was clearly not a "station" with contrived activity sheets for students to follow; rather, it encouraged talking, writing, exploration, and problem solving directed by the students. After construction, the presence of the igloo also provided plenty of natural opportunities for Ms. Hall and the children to use the vocabulary (like *arc*).

The intentional interactions Ms. Hall had with the children contributed to the rigor of the study of igloos without disrupting the children's self-directed learning and exploration. The use of effective questioning techniques enables students to consider various answers and outcomes. Infusing questions that have more than one right answer and encouraging investigation develops in learners the capacity to problem solve and persist. The language and skills Ms. Hall intentionally modeled and the peer collaboration she fostered enhanced the academic learning experience; the children's growing content knowledge, problem solving, persistence, initiative, and creativity were all mutually reinforcing.

The integration of content areas (math, science, language arts, visual arts, etc.) into the igloo project provided opportunities to engage in meaningful, academically rigorous, student-directed work. This was a shift in practice from the typical lessons these kindergartners had experienced in the past. As in classrooms across the country, the teachers in this school had previously taught subjects according to the schedule and only during those times. In contrast, the igloo project demanded an intersection of content areas and skills that could not be matched by a worksheet or a narrow lesson on one skill or in one subject area.

It is crucial to note that while these types of interactions are at times spontaneous and follow the students' lead, all are intentional. Ms. Hall planned activities linked to students' interests and provided opportunities for deeper exploration during center time. At all times, the teacher remains the engineer, infusing key skills, enhancing vocabulary, and linking to learning standards; yet students are afforded the opportunity to independently guide their learning—very often through play. Ms. Hall's ability to shift from her plan to study skyscrapers to using igloos as the means of learning exemplified the role of teacher moving fluidly from leader to guide yet remaining an intentional instructor with specific learning goals. A flexible teaching approach allows for this shift of content to support students' interests while helping them meet learning standards. This approach provides children agency in their learning and highlights their voice in the classroom community.

After the igloo project concluded, Ms. Hall reflected with the coach. Ms. Hall emphasized the students' interest in asking questions and exploring concepts and the resulting increase in their vocabulary: "The students have more vocabulary, more questioning. Now if I say a word, at least five or six will ask, 'What does that mean?' They want to know more." She considered the students' roles as active contributors to their learning and her role in providing meaningful, rigorous, appropriate opportunities for them:

> The classroom has a better atmosphere because students are more involved in deciding the learning paths in the classroom, and I ask them their opinions more often. I engage in meaningful conversations with the children about content. Before, I was asking questions with one right answer to test them; but now I am asking more *why* and *what do you think* questions, which has increased the talk in the class exponentially!

The teacher remains the engineer, infusing key skills, enhancing vocabulary, and linking to learning standards; yet students are afforded the opportunity to independently guide their learning—very often through play.

Conclusion

Many kindergarten teachers (often unwillingly and sometimes unknowingly) succumb to a counterproductive, unrealistic vision of kindergarten that includes test-focused skill development, inappropriate expectations, and misguided teaching practices. It's time for teachers, administrators, parents, and policy makers to reject that vision—especially for our learners from underresourced communities and our dual language learners. Effective kindergarten classrooms have balanced—developmentally appropriate and academically rigorous—programs in place. Departing from a didactic, controlling kindergarten curriculum is crucial for supporting all children and for offering the enriched learning experiences that are most likely to close the achievement gap. A well-rounded curriculum that puts students at the center focuses on academic language and content and on approaches to learning (e.g., persistence, collaboration, problem solving). As a field, we must swing the pendulum back toward teachers having the professional discretion to pursue academic rigor in a developmentally appropriate manner.

Authors' note: The work reported here was funded by the Henry and Marilyn Taub Foundation. Views expressed here are the authors' and do not necessarily reflect the views of the foundation.

Try This!

> I (Alexandra) responded to a child's playdough pie by introducing the vocabulary words *lattice, crust, dough, crunchy,* and *crusty.* Think of a play scenario in which you introduced one or more vocabulary words to the players. I also made a connection to my own experience baking pies with my mother. Think of a specific connection you have made to your own (or a child's) experience when teaching new vocabulary. How does doing so enrich the experience?

> Identify children's interests by noticing books they choose, activities they describe, and topics that come up often. Introduce materials, activities, and informational books to extend and add to their knowledge. Group books by themes in the reading area. Include informational books in learning and play centers and help children use them to answer questions.

> Ask thinking questions: "What can you tell me about your drawing?" or "How can you make your igloo get smaller at the top?" Questions like "How do/did you . . . ?" and "Why do you think . . . ?" encourage children to explain their thinking and ideas and form solutions to problems.

naeyc®
Accreditation
Early Learning Programs

This chapter supports the following NAEYC Early Learning Program Accreditation Standards and topic areas:

Standard 2: Curriculum
2.A Essential Characteristics
2.E Early Literacy

Standard 3: Teaching
3.A Designing Enriched Learning Environments
3.E Responding to Children's Interests and Needs
3.G. Using Instruction to Deepen Children's Understanding and Build Their Skills and Knowledge

You may be just discovering what guided play is and feeling excited to put some new plans into action. Maybe you've been thinking about different types of play—free play, guided play, and games—and how to integrate them into your teaching. Or you might wonder how beneficial and realistic it really is to try to accomplish learning goals within a child-centered environment. Maybe you're already using a playful learning approach and have seen the benefits of it. Wherever you are in your teaching journey, the children you work with will benefit from your thoughtful engagement with the ideas presented in this book and from the new play activities, materials, and strategies it might inspire you to use.

Reflection

Marie L. Masterson

Next Steps

As you revisit each chapter, what stands out? Was there something you could not wait to try? Did you have an "aha" moment about how playful learning and guided play can benefit the children you teach? What did you realize about opportunities to enrich play that you hadn't considered before?

As discussed throughout this book, guided play involves a balance of child-guided opportunities and intentional teacher support and guidance. The authors have illustrated different ways to provide that balance. You might start, then, by choosing a chapter with ideas and strategies you want to implement.

First, consider the abilities, interests, and efforts of the children you work with. Observe them to better understand how to plan meaningful learning opportunities that will help each child make connections to academic content.

Second, take a look at your play areas (including the outdoor environment) and think about the purpose of the materials currently available to the children. Think about the goals you have for learning, then make a list of informational book topics, materials, and resources that will enhance play experiences.

Next, observe children as they use the current materials. Which do they most often choose and enjoy? What can they not wait to explore? What is it about that experience that engages them? What are they saying and doing that connects to their own lives? What questions can you ask to challenge and guide their thinking? How will they end a particular play experience with greater knowledge, understanding, and skill than they had before? How can you balance child-directed and teacher-guided activities in different ways to support specific areas of development?

An Environment for Playful Learning

Use this checklist to evaluate your spaces, materials, routines, and activities; notice more details about children's experiences; and see opportunities for play through their and their families' perspectives.

- ☐ Do I know and understand each child well enough to respond meaningfully to individual abilities and needs? Do I seek to know families, viewing them as partners in their child's education?

- ☐ Do I set purposeful learning goals for materials and activities and know which areas of development and content skills will be supported?

- ☐ Do play themes, books, props, and other materials and learning opportunities support the language and cultural experiences of the children and their families?

- ☐ Do materials and conversations increase children's attention and persistence? Do I see how the activity strengthens executive function skills and self-regulation?

- ☐ Do I notice the way children's skills change over time and update materials to ensure increasingly complex challenges to keep pace with their needs? Do I share with families why we do what we do in the classroom and sincerely seek their input?

- ☐ Do I observe carefully, noticing what works well and what needs to be adjusted to foster greater engagement? Do I provide feedback that offers information or vocabulary that helps children dig deeper in understanding?

- ☐ Do I use open-ended questioning to draw children into conversations and encourage their ideas and explanations?

- ☐ Do I listen to and notice children's words, interactions with others, and emerging skills? Do I capture these through written notes, photographs, videos, and samples of children's work? Do I share the excitement of what children are learning with their families?

- ☐ Do I introduce and model rich, descriptive vocabulary in a variety of ways during play, reading, and daily activities? Do I introduce props that invite children to understand the meaning of new words and act these out during play?

- ☐ Do I encourage flexibility, empathy, cooperation, collaboration, and problem-solving skills as children engage with their peers?

- ☐ Do I reflect with my coteachers on the effectiveness of playful learning and plan action steps for positive change?

- ☐ Do I talk with families about their goals for children, ask about the child's home experiences, and invite contributions to play themes and materials?

Adapted from "20 DAP Checklist Questions for Teachers," 2016, NAEYC.org/resources/blog/20-dap-checklist-questions-teachers.

Finally, watch how children interact with each other. Think about the spaces where they play, their play themes, and what they do and say when they're together. What can you adjust to make their interactions more meaningful? How can you become a gentle guide to foster deeper, richer play? Is there anything you missed during early observations? What other opportunities do you see to build on children's skills and ideas?

Concluding Thoughts

Implementing guided play strategies may change the way your setting looks. They will change the way children engage and learn. During play, every area of children's development is enhanced; their bodies and minds are energized and focused, they learn and use new vocabulary, they plan and carry out their ideas, and they become more skilled in relating to others. You'll see children's faces light up with eagerness to explore new materials. You will hear their excited questions and gain deeper understanding of the way play strengthens their skills and their confidence. As children actively contribute to their own learning, their initiative blossoms. They begin taking responsibility for themselves and look for ways to collaborate with others. They stay at complex tasks longer and take on more difficult challenges. They grow in their ability to think critically.

Share your insights about a balanced teaching approach with families, along with the evidence you collect of how it boosts children's development.

> Seek opportunities to collaborate with other teachers and administrators; together, learn more about the role of play in children's development and celebrate the growth you see.

By advocating for play-based learning, you can help strengthen children's circles of support.

This is the goal of education in the early childhood years—to build on what children already know and can do in order to instill a love of learning and ensure strong social, emotional, physical, cognitive, and language skills that will propel them to ongoing success in school and in life.

As children actively contribute to their own learning, their initiative blossoms.

naeyc For Families

Play and Learning Go Hand in Hand

Laurel Bongiorno

Does your child's school time often look like playtime? Good! Play and learning are not separate activities for young children—they're closely connected. Teachers intentionally design play opportunities, activities, and environments with specific learning goals in mind.

Here are some of the ways play helps your child develop skills and knowledge—and sets her up for future school success.

How Play Helps Children Develop Skills and Knowledge

Cognitive Skills

Play helps children develop *cognitive skills*—thought processes of learning. These include remembering, problem solving, making decisions, processing information, and learning language. Children also learn foundational concepts and skills in math, science, and social studies.

> **Math:** When children are shoppers or cashiers in a pretend grocery store or they build in the block area, they count ("I have three pennies"), explore measurement ("This tower is not as tall as the other tower we made"), and solve problems ("Put the big blocks on the bottom so your wall won't fall down").

> **Science:** When there's a problem to solve (like making a ramp that lets cars go down faster), children make predictions, test their ideas to find a solution, and try to improve on their ideas. They develop their observation skills and understanding of natural processes as they watch seeds growing over time, and they draw and write their observations.

> **Social studies:** Children learn about themselves and the world around them by trying out different roles in their play ("Put your arm here so I can take an X-ray"). They develop plans and act on them, and they apply what they've learned to new situations.

Language and Literacy

Children develop foundational reading, vocabulary, and writing skills as they tell familiar stories to stuffed animals ("Once upon a time, there were three bears") and create a menu for their restaurant ("Write *pizza* first—it starts with *p*").

Social Skills

During play, children collaborate, negotiate, solve problems, and take turns. They learn to see things from another person's point of view and negotiate when their ideas conflict ("How about you and Danisa fix the potholes? And I'll make the stop sign and hold it.").

Emotional Skills

As children play that they're at a birthday party ("I'm really excited about blowing out the candles") or a doctor visit ("Will I get a shot? I feel scared."), they are able to focus, relax, feel successful, and express their feelings of happiness, frustration, surprise, anger, or delight. Their attention spans lengthen as they engage in play that evolves over several days. They feel confident and competent as they take on roles.

Physical Abilities

Children develop their small and large motor skills during play. They construct with different types of blocks, complete puzzles, and paint pictures (small motor). They run on the playground, dance to music, and learn to hop (large motor).

Serious Fun: How Guided Play Extends Children's Learning, edited by Marie L. Masterson and Holly Bohart. Copyright © 2019 by the National Association for the Education of Young Children. All rights reserved.

Play at Home

Toys and play materials don't need to be fancy or expensive. You've probably noticed that children can and do use just about anything as a prop for their play! And the more ways they can use an item, the more imaginative, creative, and rich their play becomes.

Here are just a few everyday items that offer lots of ways for your child to learn through play:

> **Blocks:** Cardboard boxes can be used as blocks.

> **Pretend play furniture and props:** Large cardboard boxes (microwave size or bigger) can be made into a pretend stove, a cradle, or basic child-size kitchen furniture (sink, table, refrigerator). Dolls, wooden spoons, and storage containers can be used as additional props.

> **Water toys:** Small cups, pots and pans, measuring cups and spoons, funnels, and balls can be used in the bathtub.

> **Art supplies:** Watercolor paints, washable paints, paper, crayons, markers, paintbrushes, old toothbrushes, clay, and playdough can all be used to make art.

What Teachers Do During Play

> **Observe children:** Teachers notice what each child knows and is able to do. This information helps them plan additional activities and opportunities that will support each child's learning.

> **Ask questions** that prompt children to think and to talk about their ideas: "How will you make the road signs for the highway you want to build with the blocks?"

> **Give specific feedback:** "If you move the chair, you will have more room to play."

> **Encourage children's persistence and effort,** not just what they've accomplished.

> **Create challenge** so that a task goes a bit beyond what your child can already do, like putting out a puzzle with more pieces or suggesting your child sketch an idea for the structure she wants to build with cardboard boxes.

> **Help children solve problems:** "Do you want to try the tape or the glue first to see which will work better for attaching the cotton balls to your collage?"

> **Document what children are doing and saying** to show their learning and development.

If you wonder what your child is learning from playing at school—or if the children don't seem to have many opportunities to play—talk to your child's teacher. When you share information about what your child likes to do and is good at, you and the teacher can work together to provide meaningful play and learning opportunities at home and at school.

"What Teachers Do During Play" adapted from "10 Effective DAP Teaching Strategies," NAEYC. NAEYC.org/resources/topics/dap/10-effective-dap-teaching-strategies.

Serious Fun: How Guided Play Extends Children's Learning, edited by Marie L. Masterson and Holly Bohart. Copyright © 2019 by the National Association for the Education of Young Children. All rights reserved.

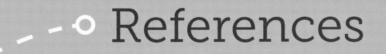

References

ACNJ (Advocates for Children of New Jersey). 2016. *Healthy Food, Strong Kids: Building a Community Response to Childhood Hunger.* Newark, NJ: ACNJ.

Adair, J.K. 2014. "Agency and Expanding Capabilities in Early Grade Classrooms: What It Could Mean for Young Children." *Harvard Educational Review* 84 (2): 217–41.

Alanís, I., & M. Arreguín-Anderson. 2015. "Developing Paired Learning in Dual Language Classrooms." *Early Years: Journal of the Texas Association for the Education of Young Children* 36 (1): 24–28.

Alfieri, L., P.J. Brooks, N.J. Aldrich, & H.R. Tenenbaum. 2011. "Does Discovery-Based Instruction Enhance Learning?" *Journal of Educational Psychology* 103 (1): 1–18.

Almon, J. 2018. "Improving Children's Health Through Play: Exploring Issues and Recommendations." Alliance for Childhood. www.allianceforchildhood.org/sites/allianceforchildhood.org/files/file/Improving _Children_s_Health_Through_Play.pdf.

Annie E. Casey Foundation. 2018. "Children in Poverty by Race and Ethnicity." Kids Count Data Center. http://datacenter.kidscount.org/data/tables/44-children-in-poverty-by-race-and-ethnicity#detailed/1/any /fal se/870,573,869,36,868/10,11,9,12,1,185,13/324,323.

Arreguín-Anderson, M., I. Salinas-González, & I. Alanís. 2018. "Translingual Play that Promotes Cultural Connections, Invention, and Regulation: A LatCrit Perspective." *International Multilingual Research Journal* 12 (4): 273–87.

Barnett, W.S., K. Jung, M.-J. Youn, & E.C. Frede. 2013. *Abbott Preschool Longitudinal Effects Study: Fifth Grade Follow-Up.* New Brunswick, NJ: National Institute for Early Education Research. http://nieer .org/wp-content/uploads/2013/11/APPLES205th20Grade.pdf.

Becker, D., M. McClelland, P. Loprinzi, & S. Trost. 2014. "Physical Activity, Self-Regulation, and Early Academic Achievement in Preschool Children." *Early Education & Development* 25 (1): 56–70.

Berry III, R.Q. 2008. "Access to Upper-Level Mathematics: The Stories of Successful African American Middle School Boys." *Journal for Research in Mathematics Education* 39 (5): 464–88.

Blake, S. 2009. "Engage, Investigate, and Report: Enhancing the Curriculum with Scientific Inquiry." *Young Children* 64 (6): 49–53.

Bowman, B.T., J.P. Comer, & D.J. Johns. 2018. "Addressing the African American Achievement Gap: Three Leading Educators Issue a Call to Action." *Young Children* 73 (2): 12–21.

Brown, C.P., B.S. Feger, & B. Mowry. 2015. "Helping Others Understand Academic Rigor in Teachers' Developmentally Appropriate Practices." *Young Children* 70 (4): 62–69. www.naeyc.org/resources/pubs/yc /sep2015/helping-others-understand-academic-rigor.

Bulotsky-Shearer, R., E. Bell, T. Carter, & S. Dietrich. 2014. "Peer Play Interactions and Learning for Low -Income Preschool Children: The Moderating Role of Classroom Quality." *Early Education and Development* 25 (6): 815–40.

Burgdorf, J., J. Panksepp, & J.R. Moskal. 2011. "Frequency-Modulated 50 kHz Ultrasonic Vocalizations: A Tool for Uncovering the Molecular Substrates of Positive Affect." *Neuroscience & Biobehavioral Reviews* 35 (9): 1831–36.

Burghardt, G.M. 2011. "Defining and Recognizing Play." In *Oxford Handbook of the Development of Play*, ed. A.D. Pelligrini, 9–18. New York: Oxford University Press.

Camp, D. 2000. "It Takes Two: Teaching with Twin Texts of Fact and Fiction." *The Reading Teacher* 53 (5): 400–408.

Carpenter, T.P., M.L. Franke, N.C. Johnson, A.C. Turrou, & A.A. Wager. 2016. *Young Children's Mathematics: Cognitively Guided Instruction in Early Childhood Education.* Portsmouth, NH: Heinemann.

Cavanaugh, D., K. Clemence, M. Teale, A. Rule, & S. Montgomery. 2017. "Kindergarten Scores, Storytelling, Executive Function, and Motivation Improved Through Literacy-Rich Guided Play." *Early Childhood Education Journal* 45 (6): 831–43.

Cervetti, G.N., & E.H. Hiebert. 2015. "The Sixth Pillar of Reading Instruction: Knowledge Development." *The Reading Teacher* 68 (7): 548–51.

Chen, L., S.R. Bae, C. Battista, S. Qin, T. Chen, T.M. Evans, & V. Menon. 2018. "Positive Attitude Toward Math Supports Early Academic Success: Behavioral Evidence and Neurocognitive Mechanisms." *Psychological Science* 29 (3): 390–402.

Christie, J.F., & K.A. Roskos. 2009. "Play's Potential in Early Literacy Development." In *Encyclopedia on Early Childhood Development,* eds. R.E. Tremblay, M. Boivin, & R.D. Peters, 1–5. Montreal, Quebec: Centre of Excellence for Early Childhood Development and Strategic Knowledge Cluster on Early Child Development. www.child-encyclopedia.com/documents/Christie-RoskosANGxp.pdf.

Clements, D.H., & J. Sarama. 2014. *Learning and Teaching Early Math: The Learning Trajectories Approach.* 2nd ed. Studies in Mathematical Thinking and Learning Series. New York: Routledge.

Clements, D.H., J. Sarama, & C. Germeroth. 2016. "Learning Executive Function and Early Mathematics: Directions of Causal Relations." *Early Childhood Research Quarterly* 36 (3): 79–90.

Cohen, L.E., & J. Emmons. 2017. "Block Play: Spatial Language with Preschool and School-Aged Children." *Early Child Development & Care* 187 (5/6): 967–77.

Connecticut State Department of Education. 2008. "Connecticut Preschool Assessment Framework Manual." www.ct.gov/oec/lib/oec/earlycare/elds/preschool_assessment_framework.pdf.

Cooper, P.M. 2005. "Literacy Learning and Pedagogical Purpose in Vivian Paley's 'Storytelling Curriculum.'" *Journal of Early Childhood Literacy* 5 (3): 229–51.

Copple, C., & S. Bredekamp. 2009. *Developmentally Appropriate Practice in Early Childhood Programs Serving Children from Birth through Age 8.* 3rd. ed. Washington, DC: NAEYC.

Dewey, J. 1897. "My Pedagogic Creed." *School Journal* 54 (3): 77–80.

Dickinson, D.K, & M.V. Porche. 2011. "Relation Between Language Experiences in Preschool Classrooms and Children's Kindergarten and Fourth-Grade Language and Reading Abilities." *Child Development* 82 (3): 870–86.

Digitale-Stanford, E. 2018. "Good Attitude about Math Gets Kid Brains in High Gear." Futurity. www.futurity.org/positive-attitude-math-brains-1665192/.

Dore, R.A., E.D. Smith, & A.S. Lillard. 2015. "How Is Theory of Mind Useful? Perhaps to Enable Social Pretend Play." *Frontiers in Psychology* 6: 1559. http://journal.frontiersin.org/article/10.3389/fpsyg.2015.01559/full.

Draper, C.L., & S. Wood. 2017. "From Stumble to STEM: One School's Journey to Explore STEM with Its Youngest Students." *Exchange* (January/February): 61–65.

Duncan, G.J., C.J. Dowsett, A. Claessens, K. Magnuson, A.C. Huston, P. Klebanov, L.S. Pagani, L. Feinstein, M. Engel, J. Brooks-Gunn, H. Sexton, K. Duckworth, & C. Japel. 2007. "School Readiness and Later Achievement." *Developmental Psychology* 43 (6): 1428–46.

Edwards, C., L. Gandini, & G. Forman, eds. 1993. *The Hundred Languages of Children: The Reggio Emilia Approach to Early Childhood Education.* Westport, CT: Ablex.

Edwards, C., L. Gandini, & G. Forman, eds. 1998. *The Hundred Languages of Children: The Reggio Emilia Approach—Advanced Reflections.* 2nd ed. Westport, CT: Ablex.

Engel, M., A. Claessens, T. Watts, & G. Farkas. 2016. "Mathematics Content Coverage and Student Learning in Kindergarten." *Educational Researcher* 45 (5): 293–300.

Espinosa, L. 2002. "From Where I Sit: Relationships and Play—Links to Language and Literacy." *Scholastic Early Childhood Today.* www.scholastic.com/teachers/articles/teaching-content/where-i-sit-relationships-and-play-links-language-and-literacy.

Farran, D.C., D. Meador, C. Christopher, K.T. Nesbitt, & L.E. Bilbrey. 2017. "Data-Driven Improvement in Prekindergarten Classrooms: Report from a Partnership in an Urban District." *Child Development* 88 (5): 1466–79.

Feeney, S., E. Moravcik, & S. Nolte. 2019. *Who Am I in the Lives of Children? An Introduction to Early Childhood Education.* 11th ed. New York: Pearson.

Fisher, K.R., K. Hirsh-Pasek, R.M. Golinkoff, D.G. Singer, & L. Berk. 2010. "Playing Around in School: Implications for Learning and Educational Policy." In *The Oxford Handbook of the Development of Play,* eds. P. Nathan & A. Pellegrini, 341–60. New York: Oxford University Press.

Fisher, K.R., K. Hirsh-Pasek, N. Newcombe, & R.M. Golinkoff. 2013. "Taking Shape: Supporting Preschoolers' Acquisition of Geometric Knowledge Through Guided Play." *Child Development* 84 (6): 1872–78.

Fitzpatrick, C., R.D. McKinnon, C.B. Blair, & M.T. Willoughby. 2014. "Do Preschool Executive Function Skills Explain the School Readiness Gap between Advantaged and Disadvantaged Children?" *Learning and Instruction* 30 (1): 25–31.

Fleer, M. 2009. "Understanding the Dialectical Relations between Everyday Concepts and Scientific Concepts within Play-Based Programs." *Research in Science Education* 39 (2): 281–306.

Friedman-Krauss, A. 2016. "How Much Can High-Quality Universal Pre-K Reduce Achievement Gaps?" *Preschool Matters Today* (blog). National Institute for Early Education Research. http://nieer .org/2016/03/31/how-much-can-high-quality-universal-pre-k-reduce-achievement-gaps.

Gillanders, C., D.C. Castro, & X. Franco. 2014. "Learning Words for Life: Promoting Vocabulary in Dual Language Learners." *The Reading Teacher* 68 (3): 213–21.

Golinkoff, R.M., & K. Hirsh-Pasek. 2016. *Becoming Brilliant: What Science Tells Us About Raising Successful Children.* Washington, DC: American Psychological Association.

González, N., L.C. Moll, & C. Amanti, eds. 2005. *Funds of Knowledge: Theorizing Practices in Households, Communities, and Classrooms.* Mahwah, NJ: Lawrence Erlbaum Associates.

Gopnik, A. 2012. "Scientific Thinking in Young Children: Theoretical Advances, Empirical Research, and Policy Implications." *Science* 337 (6102): 1623–27.

Gray, P. 2014. "Risky Play: Why Children Love It and Need It." *Psychology Today* (blog). www.psychologytoday.com/us/blog/freedom-learn/201404/risky-play-why-children-love-it-and-need-it.

Grissom, J.A., & C. Redding. 2016. "Discretion and Disproportionality: Explaining the Underrepresentation of High-Achieving Students of Color in Gifted Programs." *AERA Open* 2 (1): 1–25.

Hamlin, M., & D. Wisneski. 2012. "Supporting the Scientific Thinking and Inquiry of Toddlers and Preschoolers Through Play." *Young Children* 67 (3): 82–88.

Han, M., N. Moore, C. Vukelich, & M. Buell. 2010. "Does Play Make a Difference? How Play Intervention Affects the Vocabulary Learning of At-Risk Preschoolers." *American Journal of Play* 3 (1): 82–105.

Hassinger-Das, B., K. Hirsh-Pasek, & R.M. Golinkoff. 2017. "The Case of Brain Science and Guided Play: A Developing Story." *Young Children* 72 (2): 45–50. www.naeyc.org/resources/pubs/yc/may2017/case -brain-science-guided-play.

Hirsh-Pasek, K., & R.M. Golinkoff. 2008. "Why Play = Learning." In *Encyclopedia on Early Childhood Development,* eds. R.E. Tremblay, M. Boivin, & R.D. Peters, 1–7. Montreal, Quebec: Centre of Excellence for Early Childhood Development. www.child-encyclopedia.com/documents/Hirsh-Pasek-GolinkoffANGxp.pdf.

Hirsh-Pasek, K., J.M. Zosh, R.M. Golinkoff, J.H. Gray, M.B. Robb, & J. Kaufman. 2015. "Putting Education in 'Educational' Apps: Lessons from the Science of Learning." *Psychological Science in the Public Interest* 16 (1): 3–34.

Hoisington, C. 2010. "Picturing What's Possible—Portraits of Science Inquiry in Early Childhood Classrooms." ECRP: Beyond This Issue, Collected Papers from the SEED (STEM in Early Education and Development) Conference. http://ecrp.illinois.edu/beyond/seed/Hoisington.html.

Honomichl, R.D., & Z. Chen. 2012. "The Role of Guidance in Children's Discovery Learning." *Wiley Interdisciplinary Reviews: Cognitive Science* 3 (6): 615–22.

Horn, M., & M.E. Giacobbe. 2007. *Talking, Drawing, Writing: Lessons for Our Youngest Writers.* Portland, ME: Stenhouse.

Isenberg, J.P., & J.L. Durham. 2015. *Creative Materials and Activities for the Early Childhood Curriculum.* Hoboken, NJ: Pearson.

Kirschner, P.A., J. Sweller, & R.E. Clark. 2006. "Why Minimal Guidance During Instruction Does Not Work: An Analysis of the Failure of Constructivist, Discovery, Problem-Based, Experiential, and Inquiry-Based Teaching." *Educational Psychologist* 41 (2): 75–86.

Langford, R. 2010. "Critiquing Child-Centred Pedagogy to Bring Children and Early Childhood Educators into the Centre of a Democratic Pedagogy." *Contemporary Issues in Early Childhood* 11 (1): 113–27.

Leong, D.J., & E. Bodrova. 2012. "Assessing and Scaffolding Make-Believe Play." *Young Children* 67 (1): 28–34.

Lerkkanen, M.K., N. Kiuru, E. Pakarinen, A.M. Poikkeus, H. Rasku-Puttonen, M. Siekkinen, & J.E. Nurmi. 2016. "Child-Centered Versus Teacher-Directed Teaching Practices: Associations with the Development of Academic Skills in the First Grade at School." *Early Childhood Research Quarterly* 36 (3): 145–56.

Levine, D., & J. Ducharme. 2013. "The Effects of a Teacher-Child Play Intervention on Classroom Compliance in Young Children in Child Care Settings." *Journal of Behavioral Education* 22 (1): 50–65.

Lillard, A.S., M.D. Lerner, E.J. Hopkins, R.A. Dore, E.D. Smith, & C.M. Palmquist. 2013. "The Impact of Pretend Play on Children's Development: A Review of the Evidence." *Psychological Bulletin* 139 (1): 1–34.

Lu, C., & B. Montague. 2016. "Move to Learn, Learn to Move: Prioritizing Physical Activity in Early Childhood Education Programming." *Early Childhood Education Journal* 44 (5): 409–17.

McCrory, E., S.A. De Brito, & E. Viding. 2010. "Research Review: The Neurobiology and Genetics of Maltreatment and Adversity." *Journal of Child Psychology and Psychiatry* 51 (10): 1079–95.

McGee, E.O., & F.A. Pearman II. 2014. "Risk and Protective Factors in Mathematically Talented Black Male Students: Snapshots from Kindergarten through Eighth Grade." *Urban Education* 49 (4): 363–93.

Mulcahey, C. 2009. *The Story in the Picture: Inquiry and Artmaking with Young Children.* 2nd ed. Early Childhood Education Series. New York: Teachers College Press; Reston, VA: National Art Education Association.

NAEP (National Assessment of Educational Progress). 2015. "2015 Mathematics and Reading Assessments." The Nation's Report Card. www.nationsreportcard.gov/readingmath_2015/#?grade=4.

NAEYC. 2009. "Developmentally Appropriate Practice in Early Childhood Programs Serving Children from Birth through Age 8." Position statement. www.naeyc.org/positionstatements/dap.

NAEYC. Forthcoming a. "Advancing Equity and Diversity in Early Childhood Education." Position statement. Washington, DC: NAEYC.

NAEYC. Forthcoming b. "Professional Standards and Competencies for Early Childhood Educators." Position statement. Washington, DC: NAEYC.

NAEYC & NAECS/SDE (National Association of Early Childhood Specialists in State Departments of Education). 2003. "Early Childhood Curriculum, Assessment, and Program Evaluation: Building an Effective, Accountable System in Programs for Children Birth through Age 8." Joint position statement. www.naeyc.org/files/naeyc/file/positions/pscape.pdf.

NAEYC & NCTM (National Council of Teachers of Mathematics). 2002. Updated 2010. "Early Childhood Mathematics: Promoting Good Beginnings." Joint position statement. www.naeyc.org/files/naeyc/file/positions/psmath.pdf.

Nasir, N.S., & N. Shah. 2011. "On Defense: African American Males Making Sense of Racialized Narratives in Mathematics Education." *Journal of African American Males in Education* 2 (1): 24–45.

National Research Council. 2001. *Adding It Up: Helping Children Learn Mathematics.* Eds. J. Kilpatrick, J. Swafford, & B. Findell. Mathematics Learning Study Committee, Center for Education, Division of Behavioral and Social Sciences and Education. Washington, DC: National Academies Press.

NELP (National Early Literacy Panel). 2008. *Developing Early Literacy: A Scientific Synthesis of Early Literacy Development and Implications for Early Literacy Intervention.* Report of the National Early Literacy Panel. Washington, DC: National Institute for Literacy. https://lincs.ed.gov/publications/pdf/NELPReport09.pdf.

Neuman, S.B., T. Kaefer, & A. Pinkham. 2014. "Building Background Knowledge." *The Reading Teacher* 68 (2):145–48.

NJ ED (New Jersey Department of Education). 2017. "New Jersey Statewide Assessment Reports." www.nj.gov/education/schools/achievement.

Noble, K.G., S.M. Houston, N.H. Brito, H. Bartsch, E. Kan, J.M. Kuperman, N. Akshoomoff, D.G. Amaral, C.S. Bloss, O. Libiger, N.J. Schork, S.S. Murray, B.J. Casey, L. Chang, T.M. Ernst, J.A. Frazier, J.R. Gruen, D.N. Kennedy, P. Van Zijl, S. Mostofsky, W.E. Kaufmann, T. Kenet, A.M. Dale, T.L. Jernigan, & E.R. Sowell. 2015. "Family Income, Parental Education, and Brain Structure in Children and Adolescents." *Nature Neuroscience* 18 (5): 773–78.

NSF (National Science Foundation). 2017. *Women, Minorities, and Persons with Disabilities in Science and Engineering.* Arlington, VA: NSF. www.nsf.gov/statistics/2017/nsf17310/digest/about-this-report.

NSTA (National Science Teachers Association). 2014. "Early Childhood Science Education." Position statement. www.nsta.org/about/positions/earlychildhood.aspx.

Otto, B.W. 2014. *Language Development in Early Childhood Education.* 4th ed. Upper Saddle River, NJ: Pearson.

Paley, V.G. 1981. *Wally's Stories: Conversations in the Kindergarten.* Cambridge, MA: Harvard University Press.

Paley, V.G. 2009. "The Importance of Fantasy, Fairness, and Friendship in Children's Play: An Interview with Vivian Gussin Paley." *American Journal of Play* 2 (2): 121–38.

Paugh, A.L. 2005. "Multilingual Play: Children's Code-Switching, Role Play, and Agency in Dominica, West Indies." *Language in Society* 34 (1): 63–86.

Pellegrini, A.D. 2009. "Research and Policy on Children's Play." *Child Development Perspectives* 3 (2): 131–36.

Piaget, J. 1962. *Play, Dreams and Imitation in Childhood*. Trans. C. Gattegno & F.M. Hodgson. New York: W. W. Norton & Company.

Priebe, S.J., J.M. Keenan, & A.C. Miller. 2011. "How Prior Knowledge Affects Word Identification and Comprehension." *Reading and Writing* 7 (1): 581–86.

Ramani, G. 2012. "Influence of a Playful, Child-Directed Context on Preschool Children's Peer Cooperation." *Merrill-Palmer Quarterly* 58 (2): 159–90.

Ramani, G., & C. Brownell. 2014. "Preschoolers' Cooperative Problem Solving: Integrating Play and Problem Solving." *Journal of Early Childhood Research* 12 (1): 92–108.

Ramani, G., & S. Eason. 2015. "It All Adds Up: Learning Early Math Through Play and Games." *Phi Delta Kappan* 96 (8): 27–32.

Ranz-Smith, D.J. 2007. "Teacher Perception of Play: In Leaving No Child Behind Are Teachers Leaving Childhood Behind?" *Early Education and Development* 18 (2): 271–303.

Reeves, D.B. 2010. *Transforming Professional Development into Student Results*. Alexandria, VA: ASCD.

Riojas-Cortez, M. 2001. "Preschoolers' Funds of Knowledge Displayed Through Sociodramatic Play Episodes in a Bilingual Classroom." *Early Childhood Education Journal* 29 (1): 35–40.

Salinas-Gonzalez, I., M. Arreguín-Anderson, & I. Alanís. 2015. "Classroom Labels That Young Children Can Use: Enhancing Biliteracy Development in a Dual Language Classroom." *Dimensions of Early Childhood* 43 (1), 25–32.

Savina, E. 2014. "Does Play Promote Self-Regulation in Children?" *Early Child Development and Care* 184 (11): 1692–705.

Schickedanz, J.A., & M.F. Collins. 2013. *So Much More than the ABCs: The Early Phases of Reading and Writing*. Washington, DC: NAEYC.

Schulz, L.E., & E.B. Bonawitz. 2007. "Serious Fun: Preschoolers Engage in More Exploratory Play When Evidence Is Confounded." *Developmental Psychology* 43 (4): 1045–50.

Selmi, A.M., R. Gallagher, & E.R. Mora-Flores. 2015. *Early Childhood Curriculum for All Learners: Integrating Play and Literacy*. Los Angeles: SAGE.

Siegler, R.S. 2016. "Continuity and Change in the Field of Cognitive Development and in the Perspectives of One Cognitive Developmentalist." *Child Development Perspectives* 10 (2): 128–33.

Siegler, R.S., & G.B. Ramani. 2009. "Playing Linear Number Board Games—But Not Circular Ones—Improves Low-Income Preschoolers' Numerical Understanding." *Journal of Educational Psychology* 101 (3): 545–60.

Singer, D.G., R.M. Golinkoff, & K. Hirsh-Pasek. 2006. *Play = Learning: How Play Motivates and Enhances Children's Cognitive and Social-Emotional Growth*. New York: Oxford University Press.

Sluss, D.J. 2015. *Supporting Play in Early Childhood: Environment, Curriculum, Assessment*. 2nd ed. Stamford, CT: Cengage.

Snow, C.E. 2017. "The Role of Vocabulary Versus Knowledge in Children's Language Learning: A Fifty-Year Perspective/El papel del vocabulario frente al conocimiento en el aprendizaje lingüístico de los niños: una perspectiva de cincuenta años." *Journal for the Study of Education and Development/Infancia y Aprendizaje* 40 (1): 1–18.

Snow, C.E., & T.J. Matthews. 2016. "Reading and Language in the Early Grades." *Future of Children* 26 (1): 57–74.

Stagnitti, K., A. Bailey, E. Hudspeth Stevenson, E. Reynolds, & E. Kidd. 2016. "An Investigation into the Effect of Play-Based Instruction on the Development of Play Skills and Oral Language." *Journal of Early Childhood Research* 14 (4): 389–406.

Stipek, D., D. Clements, C. Coburn, M. Franke, & D. Farran. 2017. "PK–3: What Does It Mean for Instruction?" *Social Policy Report* 30 (2): 3–22. Washington, DC: Society for Research in Child Development. https://files.eric.ed.gov/fulltext/ED581657.pdf.

Sutton-Smith, B. 2001. *The Ambiguity of Play.* Rev. ed. Cambridge, MA: Harvard University Press.

Synodi, E. 2010. "Play in the Kindergarten: The Case of Norway, Sweden, New Zealand, and Japan." *International Journal of Early Years Education* 18 (3): 185–200.

Takanishi, R., & S. Le Menestrel, eds. 2017. *Promoting the Educational Success of Children and Youth Learning English: Promising Futures.* Report of the Academies of Sciences, Engineering, and Medicine. Washington, DC: National Academies Press.

Tayler, C. 2015. "Learning in Early Childhood: Experiences, Relationships and 'Learning to Be.'" *European Journal of Education* 50 (2): 160–74.

Tominey, S.L., & M.M. McClelland. 2011. "Red Light, Purple Light: Findings from a Randomized Trial Using Circle Time Games to Improve Behavioral Self-Regulation in Preschool." *Early Education and Development* 22 (3): 489–519.

Toub, T.S., B. Hassinger-Das, K.T. Nesbitt, H. Ilgaz, D.S. Weisberg, K. Hirsh-Pasek, R.M. Golinkoff, A. Nicolopoulou, & D.K. Dickinson. 2018. "The Language of Play: Developing Preschool Vocabulary Through Play Following Shared Book-Reading." *Early Childhood Research Quarterly* 45 (4): 1–17.

Trawick-Smith, J., S. Swaminathan, & X. Liu. 2016. "The Relationship of Teacher-Child Play Interactions to Mathematics Learning in Preschool." *Early Child Development and Care* 186 (5): 716–33.

Ursache, A., & K. Noble. 2016. "Neurocognitive Development in Socioeconomic Context: Multiple Mechanisms and Implications for Measuring Socioeconomic Status." *Psychophysiology* 53 (1): 71–82.

Van Meeteren, B., & B. Zan. 2010. "Revealing the Work of Young Engineers in Early Childhood Education." *ECRP: Beyond This Issue, Collected Papers from the SEED (STEM in Early Education and Development) Conference.* http://ecrp.uiuc.edu/beyond/seed/zan.html.

Verdine, B.N., R.M. Golinkoff, K. Hirsh-Pasek, & N.S. Newcombe. 2017. "Links Between Spatial and Mathematical Skills Across the Preschool Years." *Monographs of the Society for Research in Child Development* 82 (1): 7–126.

Vygotsky, L.S. [1930–35] 1978. *Mind in Society: The Development of Higher Psychological Processes.* Ed. and trans. M. Cole, V. John-Steiner, S. Scribner, & E. Souberman. Cambridge, MA: Harvard University Press.

Weisberg, D.S., K. Hirsh-Pasek, & R.M. Golinkoff. 2013. "Guided Play: Where Curricular Goals Meet a Playful Pedagogy." *Mind, Brain, and Education* 7 (1): 104–12. www.sas.upenn.edu/~deenas/papers/weisberg-hirshpasek-golinkoff-mbe-2013.pdf.

Weisberg, D.S., K. Hirsh-Pasek, R.M. Golinkoff, A.K. Kittredge, & D. Klahr. 2016. "Guided Play: Principles and Practices." *Current Directions in Psychological Science* 25 (3): 177–82.

Weisberg, D.S., K. Hirsh-Pasek, R.M. Golinkoff, & B.D. McCandliss. 2014. "Mise en Place: Setting the Stage for Thought and Action." *Trends in Cognitive Sciences* 18 (6): 276–78.

Weisberg, D.S., J.M. Zosh, K. Hirsh-Pasek, & R.M. Golinkoff. 2013. "Talking It Up: Play, Language Development, and the Role of Adult Support." *American Journal of Play* 6 (1): 39–54.

Wenner, M. 2009. "The Serious Need for Play." *Scientific American Mind* 20 (1): 22–29.

Willingham, D.T. 2017. "Do Manipulatives Help Students Learn?" Ask the Cognitive Scientist. *American Educator* 41 (3): 25–30, 40.

Yates, T.M., & A.K. Marcelo. 2014. "Through Race-Colored Glasses: Preschoolers' Pretend Play and Teachers' Ratings of Preschooler Adjustment." *Early Childhood Research Quarterly* 29 (1): 1–11.

Yogman, M., A. Garner, J. Hutchinson, K. Hirsh-Pasek, & R.M. Golinkoff. 2018. *The Power of Play: A Pediatric Role in Enhancing Development in Young Children.* Report of the AAP Committee on Psychosocial Aspects of Child and Family Health, AA Council on Communications and Media. *Pediatrics* 142 (3): e20182058.

Zilanawala. A., M. Martin, P.A. Noguera, & R.B. Mincy. 2017. "Math Achievement Trajectories Among Black Male Students in the Elementary- and Middle-School Years." *Educational Studies* 54 (2): 143–64.

Zosh, J.M., K. Hirsh-Pasek, E.J. Hopkins, H. Jensen, C. Liu, D. Neale, S.L. Solis, & D. Whitebread. 2018. "Accessing the Inaccessible: Redefining Play as a Spectrum." *Frontiers in Psychology* 9: 1124.

Resources for Further Learning

Introduction

Almon, J. 2018. "Improving Children's Health through Play: Exploring Issues and Recommendations." Annapolis, MD: Alliance for Childhood; Clemson, SC: US Play Coalition. https://usplaycoalition.org/wp-content/uploads/2018/04/Play-and-Health -White-Paper-FINAL.pdf

CDC (Centers for Disease Control and Prevention). 2018. "Physical Activity Facts." www.cdc.gov/healthyschools/physicalactivity/facts.htm.

NAEYC. 2018. "How Play Connects to Learning." www.naeyc.org/resources/topics/play.

Chapter 1
Brain Science and Guided Play

Brown, S., With C. Vaughn. 2009. *Play: How It Shapes the Brain, Opens the Imagination, and Invigorates the Soul*. New York: Avery.

Golinkoff, R.M., & K. Hirsh-Pasek. 2016. *Becoming Brilliant: What Science Tells Us About Raising Successful Children*. Washington, DC: American Psychological Association.

Chapter 2
Observing, Planning, Guiding: How an Intentional Teacher Meets Standards Through Play

Bodrova, E., & D.J. Leong. 2006. *Tools of the Mind: The Vygotskian Approach to Early Childhood Education*. 2nd ed. New York: Pearson.

Epstein, A.S. 2014. *The Intentional Teacher: Choosing the Best Strategies for Young Children's Learning*. Rev. ed. Washington, DC: NAEYC.

National Research Council. 2000. *How People Learn: Brain, Mind, Experience, and School*. Expanded ed. Washington, DC: National Academies Press.

Chapter 3
Supporting Language Through Culturally Rich Dramatic Play

Leong, D.J., & E. Bodrova. 2012. "Assessing and Scaffolding Make-Believe Play." *Young Children* 67 (1): 28–34.

Salinas-Gonzalez, I., M. Arreguín-Anderson, & I. Alanís. 2015. "Classroom Labels That Young Children Can Use: Enhancing Biliteracy Development in a Dual Language Classroom." *Dimensions of Early Childhood* 43 (1): 25–31.

Selmi, A.M., R. Gallagher, & E.R. Mora-Flores. 2015. *Early Childhood Curriculum for All Learners: Integrating Play and Literacy*. Los Angeles: SAGE.

Sluss, D. 2015. *Supporting Play in Early Childhood: Environment, Curriculum, Assessment*. 3rd ed. Stamford, CT: Cengage.

Chapter 4
Connecting Art, Literacy, and Drama Through Storytelling

Brooks, S. 2015. *Get into Art Telling Stories: Discover Great Art and Create Your Own!* New York: Kingfisher/Macmillan.

Caputo, J. 2009. "The 'Art' of Storytelling." Smithosonian.com. www.smithsonianmag.com/smithsonian-institution/the-art-of-storytelling-11343036.

Norfolk, S., J. Stenson, & D. Williams, eds. 2009. *Literacy Development in the Storytelling Classroom*. Santa Barbara, CA: Libraries Unlimited.

Chapter 5
Playful Math Instruction and Standards

Carpenter, T.P., M.L. Franke, N.C. Johnson, A.C. Turrou, & A.A. Wager. 2017. *Young Children's Mathematics: Cognitively Guided Instruction in Early Childhood Education*. Portsmouth, NH: Heinemann.

Franke, M.L., E. Kazemi, & A.C. Turrou. 2018. *Choral Counting & Counting Collections: Transforming the PreK–5 Math Classroom*. Portsmouth, NH: Stenhouse.

Chapter 6

Fostering Positive Experiences in the Math Center for African American Boys

Digitale-Stanford, E. 2018. "Good Attitude About Math Gets Kid Brains in High Gear." www.futurity.org/positive-attitude-math-brains-1665192.

Hughes, E. 2017. "Maintaining Engagement During Center Time." *Partnership for Developing Model Early Learning Centers* (blog). January 27. https://my.vanderbilt.edu/mnpspartnership/2017/01/engagement-during-centers-invited-blog-post.

Partnership for Developing Model Early Learning Centers. 2018. "About the 'Magic 8' Classroom Practices." Accessed December 3. https://my.vanderbilt.edu/mnpspartnership/magic8.

Willingham, D.T. 2017. "Do Manipulatives Help Students Learn?" Ask the Cognitive Scientist. *American Educator* 41 (3): 25–35, 50. www.aft.org/sites/default/files/periodicals/ae_fall2017_willingham.pdf.

Chapter 7

What Can You Do with Bamboo? Preschoolers Explore a Natural Material

Hanscom, A.J. 2016. *Balanced and Barefoot: How Unrestricted Outdoor Play Makes for Strong, Confident, and Capable Children.* Oakland, CA: New Harbinger Publications.

Kiewra, C., & E. Veselack. 2016. "Playing with Nature: Supporting Preschoolers' Creativity in Natural Outdoor Classrooms." *International Journal of Early Childhood Environmental Education* 4 (1): 71–96. https://naturalstart.org/sites/default/files/journal/10._final_kiewra_veselack.pdf.

Nature Explore. 2018. *Dimensions Educational Research Foundation.* www.natureexplore.org.

Wiedel-Lubinski, M. 2018. *7 Ways Nature-Based Learning Takes Root in Existing Preschools.* Natural Start Alliance, North American Association for Environmental Education. https://naturalstart.org/feature-stories/7-ways-nature-based-learning-takes-root-existing-preschools.

Chapter 8
Engaging and Enriching Play Is Rigorous Learning

Brown, C.P., B.S. Feger, & B. Mowry. 2015. "Helping Others Understand Academic Rigor in Teachers' Developmentally Appropriate Practices." *Young Children* 70 (4): 62–69. www.naeyc.org/resources/pubs/yc/sep2015/helping-others-understand-academic-rigor.

Gillanders, C., D.C. Castro, & X. Franco. 2014. "Learning Words for Life: Promoting Vocabulary in Dual Language Learners." *The Reading Teacher* 68 (3): 213–21.

Rendon, T., & G. Gronlund. 2017. *Saving Play: Addressing Standards Through Play-Based Learning in Preschool and Kindergarten*. St. Paul, MN: Redleaf.

Other Resources

Heroman, C. 2016. *Making and Tinkering with STEM: Solving Design Challenges with Young Children*. Washington, DC: NAEYC.

Hirsh-Pasek, K., & S. Cook. 2017. "Enhancing Knowledge and Skill Development by Gently Guiding Play" (webinar). www.youtube.com/watch?time_continue=1&v=xvMV1gf_Ibk.

Nell, M.L, & W.F. Drew. With D.E. Bush. 2013. *From Play to Practice: Connecting Teachers' Play to Children's Learning*. Washington, DC: NAEYC.

NAEYC. 2018. "Play." Accessed December 5. www.naeyc.org/resources/topics/play.

Paley, V.G. 2004. *A Child's Work: The Importance of Fantasy Play*. Chicago: The University of Chicago Press.

Strasser, J., & L.M. Bresson. 2017. *Big Questions for Young Minds: Extending Children's Thinking*. Washington, DC: NAEYC.

About the Authors and Editors

Iliana Alanís, PhD, is a professor in the Department of Interdisciplinary Learning and Teaching at the University of Texas at San Antonio. Her work focuses on teaching practices in early elementary grades, with an emphasis on the effect of schooling for language minority children in bilingual programs.

María G. Arreguín-Anderson, EdD, is an associate professor in early childhood and elementary education at the University of Texas at San Antonio. Her work illuminates the intricacies of cultural and linguistic factors that influence minority students' access to education in early childhood and elementary bilingual settings, specifically in the area of science education.

Laurel Bongiorno, PhD, is dean of the Division of Education and Human Studies at Champlain College, in Burlington, Vermont, and oversees the MEd in Early Childhood Education.

Danielle B. Davis, MPP, is a pre-K teacher in the Metro Nashville Public Schools. She served as a graduate research assistant at the Peabody Research Institute at Vanderbilt University.

Dale C. Farran, PhD, is the Antonio and Anita Gotto Chair in Teaching and Learning at Vanderbilt University, director of the Peabody Research Institute, and a member of the DREME Network. She has partnered with the Metro Nashville Public Schools Pre-K program for four years.

Alexandra Figueras-Daniel, PhD, is a senior research scientist at the Developing Language and Literacy Lab at Teachers College of Columbia University, in New York City. Her work has included numerous studies on improving outcomes for young children, with a specific focus on dual language learners.

Brenna Hassinger-Das, PhD, is an assistant professor of psychology at Pace University, in New York City. Her research examines children's play and learning in home, school, and community contexts.

Kathy Hirsh-Pasek, PhD, is the Stanley and Debra Lefkowitz Faculty Fellow in the Department of Psychology at Temple University and is a senior fellow at the Brookings Institution. She is committed to bridging the gap between research and application.

Patricia McDonald, PhD, is a mathematics instructional coach for an American school in Stuttgart, Germany. A former kindergarten teacher, she now focuses her work on assisting K–5 teachers with best practices in early childhood education and mathematics, collaborating with the community and the faculty on standards to improve learning, and advocating for play for all students.

Roberta Michnick Golinkoff, PhD, is the Unidel H. Rodney Sharp Professor of Education, Psychology, and Linguistics at the University of Delaware, in Newark. She has written numerous articles and books and lectures internationally about language development, playful learning, and spatial development.

Shannon Riley-Ayers, PhD, is a senior program officer at The Nicholson Foundation and was formerly an associate research professor at the National Institute for Early Education Research at Rutgers University, in New Jersey. Shannon's work focuses on improving outcomes for young children.

Bonnie Ripstein, MEd, is an associate professor of early childhood education at Rhode Island College, in Providence. Bonnie taught preschool and kindergarten for 14 years at the Henry Barnard Laboratory School on the Rhode Island College campus.

Irasema Salinas-Gonzalez, EdD, is an associate professor at the University of Texas Rio Grande Valley, where she teaches courses in early care and early childhood education. Her work focuses on language and literacy development of young dual language learners through play, the development of cognitive skills of dual language learners through play-based learning, and creating engaging classroom environments for young dual language learners.

Deborah Stipek, PhD, is the Judy Koch Professor of Education and the former dean of the Graduate School of Education at Stanford University. She currently directs the Heising-Simons Development and Research in Early Math Education Network (https://dreme.stanford.edu).

Condie Collins Ward is a preschool educator, artist, and writer with over 30 years' experience working with young children. She believes passionately in connecting children to the natural world. She currently teaches 4-year-olds at the Westport-Weston Cooperative Nursery School in Connecticut.

· ·

Marie L. Masterson, PhD, is director of quality assessment at McCormick Center for Early Childhood Leadership, where she oversees evaluation for the Illinois quality rating and improvement system. Marie is an educational consultant to state departments of education, schools, child care programs, and social service and parenting organizations. She is a national speaker, child behavior expert, researcher, and author of multiple books and articles that address behavior guidance, early care and education, parenting, and high-quality teaching.

Holly Bohart is senior editor in Books and Related Resources at NAEYC. She formerly taught in special education early childhood programs.

NAEYC's Bestselling Books

Great Books for Preschool and Kindergarten Teachers

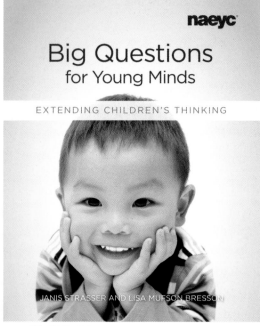

Item 1132 • 2017 • 160 pages

Big Questions for Young Minds

Questions are powerful tools, especially in the classroom. Asking rich, thoughtful questions can spark young children's natural curiosity and illuminate a whole new world of possibility and insight. But what are "big" questions, and how do they encourage children to think deeply? With this intentional approach—rooted in Bloom's Taxonomy—teachers working with children ages 3 through 6 will discover how to meet children at their individual developmental levels and stretch their thinking. With the guidance in this book as a cornerstone in your day-to-day teaching practices, learn how to be more intentional in your teaching, scaffold children's learning, and promote deeper understanding.

Finally, a resource to help teachers develop and ask questions that encourage children to think, imagine, and generate ideas!
—Beth G.

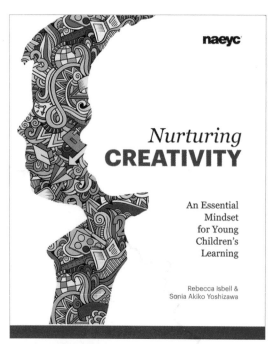

Item 1129 • 2016 • 176 pages

Nurturing Creativity

Creativity is a cornerstone of complex, unconventional thinking, and developing creativity begins at a young age. Early childhood teachers have the opportunity to inspire children's innovative thinking and doing by

› Including creative opportunities across all domains of learning
› Designing a beautiful space that encourages children's experimentation and play
› Extending children's learning and challenging their thinking
› Documenting children's thought processes and displaying their work
› Involving families and the community in children's creative endeavors
› Reflecting on your beliefs and practices about creativity and nurturing your own creativity

Use this resource to shape your classroom into a place where children problem solve, explore solutions, and try new ideas.

Watch a recorded webinar about the importance of creativity presented by the authors of this book at NAEYC.org/recorded-webinars

Item 1130 • 2017 • 144 pages

Making & Tinkering With STEM

Explore science, technology, engineering, and math (STEM) concepts through making and tinkering! With 25 classroom-ready engineering design challenges inspired by children's favorite books, educators can seamlessly integrate making and tinkering and STEM concepts in preschool through third grade classrooms. Challenge children to use everyday materials and STEM concepts to design and build solutions to problems faced by characters in their favorite books. This practical, hands-on resource includes

› 25 engineering design challenges appropriate for children ages 3–8
› Suggestions for creating a makerspace environment for children
› A list of 100 picture books that encourage STEM-rich exploration and learning
› Questions and ideas for expanding children's understanding of STEM concepts

Item 7226 • 2015 • 112 pages

Exploring Math & Science in Preschool

What every preschool teacher needs! Filled with practical strategies and useful information on math and science, including

› Learning center ideas
› Engaging activities
› Ideas that support the development and learning of every preschooler
› Children's book recommendations

This excellent resource of engaging math and science learning experiences for preschoolers was developed for you by the editors of *Teaching Young Children*.

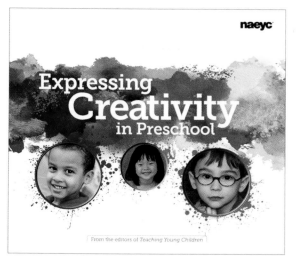

Item 7225 • 2015 • 128 pages

Expressing Creativity in Preschool

What every preschool teacher needs! Filled with practical strategies and useful information on art, music and movement, and dramatic play, this book offers

› Learning center ideas
› Engaging activities
› Practical suggestions that are easy to implement
› Ideas that support the development and learning of every preschooler
› Children's book recommendations

This excellent resource of engaging learning experiences for preschoolers was developed for you by the editors of *Teaching Young Children*.

Order online at
NAEYC.org/shop
or 1-800-424-2460

Discover NAEYC!

The National Association for the Education of Young Children (NAEYC) promotes high-quality early learning for all young children, birth through age 8, by connecting early childhood practice, policy, and research. We advance a diverse, dynamic early childhood profession and support all who care for, educate, and work on behalf of young children.

NAEYC members have access to award-winning publications, professional development, networking opportunities, professional liability insurance, and an array of members-only discounts.

Accreditation—NAEYC.org/accreditation

Across the country, **NAEYC Accreditation of Early Learning Programs** and **NAEYC Accreditation of Early Childhood Higher Education Programs** set the industry standards for quality in early childhood education. These systems use research-based standards to recognize excellence in the field of early childhood education.

Advocacy and Public Policy—NAEYC.org/policy

NAEYC is a leader in promoting and advocating for policies at the local, state, and federal levels that expand opportunities for all children to have equitable access to high-quality early learning. NAEYC is also dedicated to promoting policies that value early childhood educators and support their excellence.

Global Engagement—NAEYC.org/global

NAEYC's Global Engagement department works with governments and other large-scale systems to create guidelines to support early learning, as well as early childhood professionals throughout the world.

Professional Learning—NAEYC.org/ecp

NAEYC provides face-to-face training, technology-based learning, and Accreditation workshops—all leading to improvements in the knowledge, skills, and practices of early childhood professionals.

Publications and Resources—NAEYC.org/publications

NAEYC publishes some of the most valued resources for early childhood professionals, including award-winning books, *Teaching Young Children* magazine, and *Young Children*, the association's peer-reviewed journal. NAEYC publications focus on developmentally appropriate practice and enable members to stay up to date on current research and emerging trends, with information they can apply directly to their classroom practice.

Signature Events—NAEYC.org/events

NAEYC hosts three of the most important and well-attended annual events for educators, students, administrators, and advocates in the early learning community.

NAEYC's Annual Conference is the world's largest gathering of early childhood professionals.

NAEYC's Professional Learning Institute is the premier professional development conference for early childhood trainers, faculty members, researchers, systems administrators, and other professionals.

The **NAEYC Public Policy Forum** provides members with resources, training, and networking opportunities to build advocacy skills and relationships with policymakers on Capitol Hill.